Reader Reviews on the Juggernaut App

'Five stars for the writing, the manner in which the life of a fighter, a role model for women was conveyed. True or not, the girl's story, the lady's story, the woman's story to the leader's story that she has become will be a motivator to all females who wish to fight out in this tough world especially in the context of Indian society as an actress, a politician and a loved leader as Amma.'—**Karthikeyan**

'Dear Vaasanthi, it was a delightful reading, I finished in one sitting… Racy reading it was. Congrats. Warm regards.'
—**Sheilu Sreenivasan**

'Very gripping read. I wish the biography written by the author also gets published soon.'—**Ayshwaria**

'A snapshot of Jayalalithaa's life. The initial years of her life have been described well…'—**Maitri Porecha**

'A wealth of information on TN politics…'—**Shripath Shankar**

'A very informative primer on the history of Jayalalithaa. But for the occasional lapse of fair treatment, there is little bias. I would love a similar book on Karunanidhi.'—**Aroon Deep**

'A good introduction to Amma. The stories about her early life were very interesting…'—**Ruchik**

'Gives the story of Jayalalithaa… Great read on her early life and rise.'—**Alok Prasanna Kumar**

'Good and crisp writing that makes you keep on reading till the last page. A roller coaster life of a mass leader has been told without exaggeration.'—**Manoj**

'Very concisely written. At times felt that some more information was required on a subject. But nevertheless a good source for non-Tamilians to understand the intricacies of power in Tamil Nadu.'—**Subhajit**

'Fascinating. The earlier bits about Jayalalithaa, her youth and her relationship with MGR are the best ones… Definitely the most definitive read on Amma's life.'—**Ramakrishnan Mohan**

'An amazing political journey!!'—**Ronak**

Amma

Jayalalithaa's Journey from Movie Star to
Political Queen

Vaasanthi

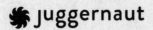

JUGGERNAUT BOOKS

KS House, 118 Shahpur Jat, New Delhi 110049, India

First published by Juggernaut Books 2016

10 9 8 7 6 5 4 3 2

ISBN 9788193284148

Typeset in Adobe Caslon Pro by R. Ajith Kumar, New Delhi

Printed at Manipal Technologies Ltd

Contents

Contents

Acknowledgements

I first met Jayalalithaa way back in 1984 in Delhi, when she was a Rajya Sabha member. With her good looks and her fluent English, she impressed even senior MPs like Khushwant Singh with her maiden speech. A friend of mine, Rajendra Awasthi, editor of *Kadambini*, the popular Hindi magazine of the *Hindustan Times* group, asked me to interview Jayalalithaa who was staying at Tamil Nadu House.

The first thing that struck me was her simple and elegant attire, and the fact that she wore no make-up. One could hardly believe that she had once been the most sought-after glamour queen of the South Indian film world. She impressed me too with her brisk professional demeanour and her sharp and aggressive answers. She seemed very sure of herself. At the time I never imagined that she, a Brahmin, would find acceptance as the leader of a Dravidian party that had its roots in a movement that denounced Brahmins; nor that she would become the chief minister not once but four times, successfully challenging the core culture of mainstream Tamil Nadu politics.

I had the opportunity to watch her closely for ten years when I moved to Chennai in 1993, as editor of the Tamil edition of *India Today*. The new culture in Chennai, with her towering cutouts all over the city, seemed bizarre to me, an outsider. The more I watched her, the more intriguing she appeared. She could be ruthlessly efficient and disarmingly vulnerable; she was deified and demonized, invoking both adoration and fear.

I wanted to unravel the enigma that is Jayalalithaa. Hence this book. I have only tried to decipher her many-layered personality. She is too complex and reserved to reveal herself fully.

Acknowledgements

A special thanks to my friend K.S. Radhakrishnan, who provided me with a lot of source material from his personal collection – an incredible archive of newspaper clippings and journals. He also introduced me to Solai (who is no more), who was Jayalalithaa's speech writer when she was the AIADMK's propaganda secretary. I am grateful to Solai for sharing information that gave me a deeper insight into her inner psyche. I must thank R.M. Veerappan for explaining why he thought it was his 'moral duty' to destroy her 'evil force'.

I am also most grateful to Film News Anandan (he died recently) for his fond and frank reminiscences of Jayalalithaa. My special thanks to Srimathi and Chandini Bhulani, Jayalalithaa's classmates in Church Park Convent, for their graphic accounts of their days spent together. These offered me valuable insights into a formative period of Jayalalithaa's life. I thank all my fellow journalists who generously shared their knowledge and experiences with me.

Vaasanthi

19 May 2016

Preface

She is enigmatic. She is imperious. She is adored and she is feared. She is deified by her admirers and reviled by her opponents. When she's up in the sky in her helicopter her devotees fall on the ground and prostrate, just as they would in her presence. She stands apart, unreal and gigantic, just like those cut-out hoardings that her party workers have erected along the streets of Tamil Nadu.

During her election campaigns, crowds throng to see her, waiting for hours under the scorching sun, thirsty and hungry, to hear her speak from a faraway canopied dais where she sits regally, resplendent in her green sari, fanned by air coolers. They voted her to power four times, and she in return showered on them her numerous welfare schemes, all of them carrying her name. 'Amma' is written on every household article – the grinder, the mixie, the rice bag, the laptop, the cycle and the water bottles. Even the goats and cows are gifts from her. Love her or hate her, Amma looms large in the lives of the people of Tamil Nadu…

The transformation of J. Jayalalithaa from a glamour queen to a formidable politician is one of the most extraordinary stories of Indian politics. It's a story that needs to be told, all the more so because it is also the story of how a woman transforms herself to survive and then become all-powerful in a male-dominated society.

Ammu

Ammu was less than two years old when they brought her father Jayaram home, dead. That dark, sad night remains vivid still in Jayalalithaa's memory, haunting her at times of despair throughout her turbulent life.

A life that began with extraordinary beauty and brilliance and was then suddenly tossed into a rough ocean where demons of various hues lurked, turning the innocent little Ammu into Amma, a woman of steel.

~

After her husband's death, Jayaram's widow Veda had no option but to move with her two little children, her son Pappu and her daughter Ammu – everyone at home called Jayalalithaa by that pet name – to her father's house in Bangalore. Rangaswamy Iyengar, a Brahmin hailing originally from Srirangam in Tamil Nadu, settled in Bangalore when he got a modest job at Hindustan Aeronautics Limited. The family was known for its good looks and very fair skin. He had three very pretty daughters, Veda, Ambuja and Padma, and a son, Srinivasan. It was a typical orthodox, conservative Brahmin middle-class household with its daily rituals and prayers diligently performed by Rangaswamy Iyengar and his wife, Kamalamma.

The young and beautiful Veda, eager to provide for her children, took up a secretarial job at the Income Tax Office to ease the additional financial burden on her father. Soon, however, she realized that on her meagre earnings she could provide her children with no more than the bare necessities. Then Kempraj Urs, a Kannada film producer, spotted Veda and was struck by her beauty. He wanted to cast her in his new film.

When he came to ask her father's permission, a furious Iyengar sent him away.

Veda's youngest sister, Padma, was still studying in college. The other sister, Ambuja, was a rebel. She became an air hostess and the horrified Iyengar promptly declared that his second daughter was dead. Ambuja was undaunted. She took to acting in films, changed her name to Vidhyavathi and set up house in Chennai. Ambuja asked Veda to come and stay with her, so that her children could go to a better school. It was an offer Veda could not resist and she and her children moved to Ambuja's house. The children were put in school, but the producers who came to meet Vidhyavathi found that Veda too had film star looks. They persuaded her to become an actor and, seeing what a comfortable life her sister led, Veda decided that that was the only way she could become prosperous enough to give her children a good life. Kempraj Urs again offered her a role and soon Veda, now renamed Sandhya, became a busy star.

A new phase in Ammu's life, marked by turbulent upheavals, was about to begin.

A Lonely Childhood

Sandhya soon realized that it was quite impossible to take care of the children with her busy acting schedule, so she sent her children back to her parents' house in Bangalore. Little Ammu yearned constantly for her mother. The children would eagerly wait for Sandhya's brief visits, when she would arrive laden with gifts and sweets. Both children loved reading, and she bought them loads of story books, to distract them from crying when she left for Chennai.

Ammu settled into her new school in Bangalore, Bishop Cotton, where she spent four years. Then came another upheaval. Their aunt Padma, who used to take care of Ammu and Pappu, got married and moved away, so Sandhya decided to bring her children back to Chennai. Jayalalithaa was thrilled to be with her mother again. But she soon realized that Sandhya was busier than ever, and had little time to spend with them. The longing for her mother's company never left Jayalalithaa.

She was ten when she joined the prestigious Church Park Convent in Chennai. Excellent at her studies, and with beautiful manners, she soon became a favourite of all the teachers, while her fellow students admired her for her striking good looks. She had a peachy pink complexion that was unusual for a south Indian, long, shining hair and beautiful eyes. That she was an actress's daughter gave her an added aura of glamour.

While the accolades at school made her happy and confident, Jayalalithaa was deeply unhappy that Sandhya was never there to share her joys and her worries. She later wrote in her memoirs that once, after not seeing her mother for two days, she had stayed up late the next night to show her an essay she had written titled 'My Mother: What She Means to Me'. The essay had won a prize and the teacher was so pleased with it that she had read it out to all the students. When Sandhya arrived late that night she saw her daughter fast asleep, with a notebook spread across her chest. As she tried to lift her up, Jayalalithaa woke up and, between tears, said how she had waited for two days to show her the essay. Sandhya sat with her and asked her to read out the essay. 'She patted my cheeks and kissed me saying that it was a beautiful essay. She hugged me and said, "Sorry, I kept you waiting, it will not happen again."'

But it happened again and again. Waiting for mother became a habit. Along with it grew disappointment and resentment. And she hated the sight of the film producers and actors who came to the house at odd hours. As if to escape from an atmosphere she found repugnant, she devoured every book she came across. She had dreams of becoming a doctor or a lawyer. Or if she were lucky, enter the Indian Administrative Service. But she was determined to stay far from the cine world.

~

Jayalalithaa realized early that there was a stigma attached to the profession. No one respected an actress, no matter how hard she worked or how successful she was. Sandhya and her children lived on Sivagnanam street in Thiyagaraya Nagar. When Jayalalithaa was thirteen, a girl who lived two houses away befriended her. She too was a student at Church Park Convent, two years her senior, and little Ammu was proud of this friendship because seniors usually maintained a distance from the juniors. Jayalalithaa was happy to have some company in the evenings after she came back from school. The two girls liked to go up to the terrace to chat.

Jayalalithaa was not aware that her friend came up there so often only to silently communicate from the terrace with her boyfriend, the son of a Jain businessman. The boy would stand on his terrace two houses away at the end of the road. Jayalalithaa, noticing her friend's antics, asked her one day what was going on. The girl confessed that she was in love with the boy and asked her not to disclose this to her parents. She also requested Jayalalithaa to signal to the boy on the days she was not able to visit. Jayalalithaa was thrilled to be privy to such a secret, and to be the go-between in this romance. The girl did not come the next day. When the boy did not see her he signalled Jayalalithaa asking where she was. Jayalalithaa signalled back that she had not come.

The milk vendor who supplied milk to the lane saw this dumb charade that day and then again the next day. She hurried to the girl's house and warned her parents not to send their daughter to an actress's house – the actress's daughter was clearly a flirt and would spoil their daughter's reputation.

The girl stopped coming and Jayalalithaa, unaware of what had happened, went to her house to find out why. She was shocked when the girl refused to let her in because of what the milk seller had said. 'She has said that you introduced me to that boy and spoilt me.' The girl's mother, scowling and looking at Jayalalithaa accusingly, was standing behind her. Jayalalithaa wanted to protest, but then realized that the girl didn't have the guts to tell her mother the truth and instead was ready to make her the scapegoat.

Jayalalithaa was both shocked and deeply hurt. She wrote in her memoirs: 'I realized what the word "betrayal" really meant. I tried to help that girl in all innocence. I thought even to stand before her was a disgrace for me. I ran to my house, sat on the terrace all by myself and wept for a couple of hours. It was a humiliating experience. I never told my mother about this.'

Sandhya had initially never considered a film career for her daughter. But she did want her daughter to become a good dancer. As soon as Ammu came back from Bangalore to Chennai, she was put under the tutelage of K.J. Sarasa, a reputed dance teacher in those days. Jayalalithaa, who later blossomed into a good dancer, was not keen to learn dance.

But Sarasa was a very patient and persuasive teacher and trained her well enough for her to have her arangetram when she was barely twelve years old, in May 1960. A number of film dignitaries turned up to see Sandhya's daughter's debut performance, including leading actors, actresses and producers. Sivaji Ganesan, the most talented actor of that time, presided over the function. He praised Jayalalithaa's performance and said she was as lovely as a golden statue. 'I wish that she blossoms into a very popular film star.' Jayalalithaa and Sandhya were happy with his words but did not take them seriously. Both were determined that Jayalalithaa should not join the film world. Nor could Sivaji have imagined that this chit of a girl with 'laddoo cheeks' would one day act with him as his heroine.

~

Srimathi, Jayalalithaa's classmate and close friend until she joined politics, has many anecdotes about their student days. She recalls: 'It was an unwritten code that all girls from Church Park would go to Stella Maris college. So we also decided to go to Stella. Jayalalithaa used to say she'd join the IAS or do medicine. She had great hopes for her academic future. So when her mother took her along to film shoots she'd protest, though not vociferously because she was by nature a well-behaved girl.' Jayalalithaa often told Srimathi that she did not like the film-world atmosphere, and that the men there were crude and stared at her lustfully.

'Jaya would say, "When I go home these rascals will be sitting there. I get so annoyed seeing them – all kinds of men, tall, short, dark, fair, thin and fat and oily! Mother asks me to sit with them and talk. I hate it."' She said this with a vehemence that Srimathi still remembers. It was obvious that Jayalalithaa felt she was being forced into doing things that went against her nature. Perhaps she also yearned for a normal family life like her other classmates had.

Srimathi recalls that while her mother or father came to pick her up from school, Jayalalithaa's car most often came late. 'So I would wait along with her till her car came. I remember an incident during our matriculation exams. We had to go to Lady Wellington college to write the exams. We collected our exam tickets from school and waited for our cars, standing outside the school. But her car never came. When my father came to pick me up, he offered to drop her also, as she'd otherwise miss the exam. My father was a still photographer in film studios and she knew him. She hesitated but then came along. She never forgot this simple act. She would talk about it with great emotion: "Had it not been for your father I would not have been able to write my exams." She would say, "Look, nobody bothered in my house." She got the best outgoing student shield in school. She came second in the state. Even then nobody came from her house to the school award function.'

Srimathi continues, 'She was very keen on joining college. But even before the admissions started, she was by some quirk of fate already knee-deep in the film world and was busy shooting *Aayiraththil Oruvan*. So she asked me to get the form and fill it up with the same subject group I had opted for. I opted for fine arts, and I filled her form with the same choices and paid the fees. She came on the first day of college. Stella Maris was a very strict institution. Jayalalithaa came to the class with nothing in her hand – no notebook or textbooks. Sushila Mary, the lecturer, knew nothing about Jayalalithaa. She asked Jaya some question. Jaya said she didn't have the book. The lecturer got very angry. She started scolding Jaya and the words poured out like a torrent: "Why do you come to class then

– just to dress like a doll?" Jaya went home for lunch and never came back. I called her and asked why she had disappeared like that. She said she could not cope with that kind of place. I said she could try going to some other college. She then said that she realized that pursuing both acting and studies was impossible.'

She was indeed too busy to do both at that time – she was acting in her first film with MGR, the man who was to completely alter the course of her life, for better and for worse.

Jayalalithaa had plunged almost unthinkingly into another world, not aware that it was a world of dreams and frustration, of schemers and manipulators, of demons and gods...

A Star Is Born

So how did Jayalalithaa, who was so determined to stay away from the film world, find herself sucked into it when she was yet in her teens?

When she took her first small step into that world, she did not know that it was an iron mesh she had walked into and there was no escaping from its intricate coils.

It was the Hundredth Day celebration for the film *Karnan*, in which Sandhya had acted. Jayalalithaa's matriculation exams were over and she was on a two-month break before college started. Sandhya took

Jayalalithaa along with her, wearing a sari for the first time. The guests at Hotel Woodlands were astonished to see that Sandhya's daughter had blossomed into a ravishing beauty.

When they were about to leave, B.R. Panthulu, the producer and host, asked them to wait as he wanted to have a word with Sandhya. He told her he was starting shooting the following week for his new Kannada film, and he wanted to cast her daughter as the heroine. Both mother and daughter were taken aback. Sandhya, till then firm that her daughter should not enter the film world, muttered that Jayalalithaa had to join college in two months. Panthulu assured her that the shooting would be over by then. Sandhya, expecting a protest from her daughter, turned to her and asked her what she thought about it. To her mother's surprise Jayalalithaa said, 'Yes!'

Perhaps she thought it would be an amusing way to pass the two months between school and college. After that fateful encounter with Panthulu, however, Jayalalithaa barely had time to think about the impulsive decision she had taken. She had to leave for Mysore immediately, where shooting would begin at the Brindavan Gardens.

'Film News' Anandan, who wrote for *Film News* and later worked as Jayalalithaa's public relations officer (PRO), recounts an incident in Mysore that marked Jayalalithaa as remarkably fearless even when she was barely sixteen.

'She belonged to the Mandiam Iyengar community that hailed from Karnataka. But in an article that appeared in a magazine she was quoted as saying, "I am a Tamilian. My mother belongs to Srirangam." That angered the Kannadigas in Karnataka who believed her to be a Kannadiga. Because of the threats she received she cancelled her scheduled dance programme at the Dasara arts festival in Mysore. Two months later, during the shooting of director Panthulu's film at the Chamundi studios in Mysore, the organizer of the Dasara arts festival heard she was there, and decided to confront her. The studio manager got news that about a hundred protesters were marching towards the studio to beat up Jayalalithaa. So he ordered the gates to be locked. But the hooligans jumped over the gates and entered with lathis in their hands shouting in Kannada: "Where is the bitch?" They barged in, knocking down the guards and journalists standing at the door. Panthulu spoke to them in Kannada and pleaded with them to go away. But they demanded that Jayalalithaa should say sorry for having said that she was not a Kannadiga. Jayalalithaa was neither ruffled nor afraid. She looked straight at them and said in chaste Kannada, "I have not said anything wrong. Why should I apologize? I am a Tamilian and not a Kannadiga!"

'By then the police entered and pacified the protesters and took them away. That Kannadigas attempted to kill Jayalalithaa hit the headlines in all Tamil papers.'

~

For Jayalalithaa her first film shoot in Mysore was fun, but after she returned to Chennai she did not dwell on it. For she had received a letter from the education ministry, offering her a scholarship for further studies, because of her brilliant performance in the state's matriculation exam. She was thrilled by this letter and was all set to proceed with her plans for higher studies. But just then there was an offer for a heroine's role in a film that was to be made by Sridhar, a reputed director. When Sandhya said that it would be foolish to refuse Sridhar's plum offer, an angry Jayalalithaa resisted.

Many years later in an interview Jayalalithaa recalled, 'I created a storm at home. I fought, I wept, I raged, but it had to be films.' She had to give in because Sandhya confessed that they were actually not 'as well off as I thought or she made us kids believe by the luxurious lifestyle she had accustomed us to'. Sandhya now had very little work coming her way, and her savings had dwindled.

After a sleepless night Jayalalithaa realized she could not refuse her mother, who had toiled so hard to make their life comfortable. And once it was decided that her future lay in films and that she should abandon her scholastic dreams, she steeled herself to put her best into the career that had been thrust on her. In an interview she elaborated, 'I couldn't be indifferent, because I have this in me – once I take up a job I will never do it half-heartedly or indifferently even if it is something like giving a bath to my dog! It was the same with acting in films. There was no intermediate or struggling period for me. Overnight I was famous and fabulously successful, the lead heroine in two languages, Tamil and Telugu.'

She concluded the interview saying, 'I can will myself to do anything in this world.' That was the mantra that she held on to through the vicissitudes of her life.

～

While she was acting in Sridhar's film she was booked again by the director Panthulu, for *Aayiraththil Oruvan* in which she was cast opposite the matinee idol MGR who was more than thirty-five years her senior. She was just sixteen. One day, during the shooting, MGR who was shooting on another floor dropped in, along with a crowd of followers. Sridhar asked her to come forward and greet MGR. When she stood before him with folded hands MGR must have been astonished to see that this schoolgirl was to be his co-star.

The very first scene that she had to do with MGR happened to be the 'first night' bedroom scene. She was embarrassed and terribly nervous. When the soundtrack of the song 'Are you shy?' came on, she was actually shivering with fright. MGR had to use all his charms to put her at ease.

But the next day the film unit was shocked to see the same girl sitting in a chair, engrossed in a book, and not bothering to greet the senior artistes when they arrived. Panthulu, a stickler for the etiquette followed in the film industry, asked Sandhya to teach her daughter how to behave. Jayalalithaa was furious with her mother, and declared that if she had to follow these rules and conventions, she was not going to continue with the film shoot. But of course she had to come round.

Jayalalithaa wrote later that there were constant fights between her and her mother but in the end it was always Sandhya who had her way – Jayalalithaa knew that she was now her mother's sole support.

Her brother Pappu (Jayakumar) had health problems and was not able to attend school regularly. Years later Jayalalithaa suddenly broke her ties with Pappu, who moved to another house with his wife and children.

None of Jayalalithaa's friends or her PROs know anything about her relationship with her brother, who has now passed away. Srimathi says, 'She never discussed her family with us. He was never present during her birthday parties either.' It is strange because in her incomplete memoirs, which were serialized in the journal *Kumudam*, she writes very fondly of her childhood pranks with her brother in Bangalore and later in Chennai.

~

Slowly Jayalalithaa learnt the protocol followed in the film world. She would greet all the seniors, don her make-up and retire to a corner with a book in hand till she was called for the next shot. When *Aayiraththil Oruvan* was being filmed, the anti-Hindi agitation was on the boil in Tamil Nadu. All the cadres and members

21

of the Dravida Munnetra Kazhagam (DMK), including MGR and other actors, were expected to participate in it. But fearing that the Tamil film industry would be greatly affected by their absence, C.N. Annadurai, president of the party, allowed them to continue with their shooting schedules. *Aayiraththil Oruvan* was partly shot in a small island near Karwar in Karnataka. One day when she was accidentally left stranded in Goa, where the film unit stayed she, hardly seventeen, astonished the others by finding her way to the island by hopping on to a passing fisherman's catamaran.

Aayiraththil Oruvan was a runaway success. It ensured that MGR and Jayalalithaa would become the most popular pair of the time, he in his early fifties and she in her teens.

Many in the film industry also noticed, some with fear and others with disapproval, MGR's growing attachment to Jayalalithaa. While many preferred not to comment about it because MGR was too powerful a figure, there was among them a snake in the grass – R.M. Veerappan, MGR's close aide and film producer, who was bent on breaking up the relationship at any cost, saying that he needed to protect MGR from an evil called Jayalalithaa. He projected Jayalalithaa as a temptress, little knowing that MGR's feelings towards her went far deeper, though for political reasons he could not make them public. If MGR was obsessed with the convent-educated lass who could have been his daughter, it became an obsession with RMV to destroy this relationship. In the face of Veerappan's hostility, Jayalalithaa felt alone and vulnerable.

Her Hero MGR

'R.M. Veerappan had an antipathy towards Jayalalithaa that had no basis at all,' said Films News Anandan. 'She was definitely not flirtatious or pushy in her behaviour towards MGR or any producer. She was very disciplined and maintained her dignity.'

But MGR openly demonstrated that he had a soft corner for Jayalalithaa. He insisted that she should be cast opposite him in all his films. When RMV refused, MGR kept him waiting for shoots and delayed the production indefinitely. When Jayalalithaa was shooting with MGR for *Adimaippen* in the Thar desert, she was the slave girl and the shot required her to be barefoot. As all the other members of the unit were in their shoes they did not realize that the sand was getting hotter by the minute. After a while a barefoot Jayalalithaa could no longer endure the burning sand and noticing her discomfort MGR ordered the unit to pack up. But Jayalalithaa's ordeal did not end there. She had to walk a long distance to the car park. 'It was sheer hell,' she said in an interview later. 'I couldn't put a step forward and I was on the verge of collapse. I never said a word, but MGR must have sensed my agony. He suddenly came from behind and swept me up in his arms. He is a hero off screen too.'

There was yet another incident which left her eternally grateful to him. After a bout of drastic dieting Jayalalithaa fainted at home. Her manager contacted MGR, who arrived promptly and arranged for her to be taken to a nursing home. The departure was delayed as everyone was waiting for Jayalalithaa's aunts who were staying in her house to accompany her to the hospital. MGR went in and found them in her bedroom fighting over who would take control of Jayalalithaa's keys. MGR took the keys away from them

– and handed them to a groggy Jayalalithaa when she recovered consciousness in the nursing home. While the incident which revealed that she could not trust her own family members was a psychological blow, MGR's tender concern for her well-being touched her deeply, all the more so because her mother had died, leaving her feeling alone and orphaned at the age of twenty-one.

When she had to travel by road at night MGR would arrange for an escort vehicle. After a stone-throwing incident at Jayalalithaa's house, he is said to have ordered a special contingent of security personnel to be posted at her house.

~

The tumultuous ups and downs in her relationship with MGR started in the early 1970s when MGR increasingly began to act with younger heroines like Latha and Manjula, thanks to the dogged perseverance of RMV. MGR also got preoccupied with politics as he was the DMK party treasurer in Karunanidhi's government. Then serious differences arose between him and Karunanidhi, but according to RMV even this was because of Jayalalithaa's influence.

MGR and Karunanidhi had once been close. When C.N. Annadurai died Nedunjezhian, the senior-most, was expected to succeed him. But MGR strongly recommended Karunanidhi's name and through his influence over party workers got him elected to the post. Karunanidhi, however, threatened by MGR's popularity, cleverly excluded him when he formed the cabinet and made him the treasurer of the DMK party.

Film News Anandan, who was closely associated with Jayalalithaa as her PRO at that time (she was the first south Indian actor to appoint a PRO on a regular salary), believed that people around MGR were jealous of her fame and proximity to MGR. 'I know when I was her PRO, MGR's car would come to fetch her at one o'clock in the afternoon. She would go for an hour and come back.' Jayalalithaa was then building her house in Poes Garden. When it was complete, the entire film industry turned up for the house-warming function except for MGR. Everyone was surprised at his absence because rumours about their liaison abounded.

Anandan said, 'Next morning she had to go to Kashmir for shooting. She boards the plane and finds MGR in the next seat! MGR also had a shooting schedule in Kashmir, but Jayalalithaa was acting with Sivaji Ganesan in another film. The two locations were 40 miles apart. But after reaching Kashmir MGR took her along with him and would send her to her shooting location 40 miles away. Jayalalithaa could have had no say in the matter. If MGR says something, it had to be done.'

But after a while Jayalalithaa found MGR overbearing and dominating. He started controlling all her activities including the clothes she wore. He even took control over her finances and she had to depend on his good mood for its release. She felt stifled and wanted to break free.

A major clash occurred between the two when she refused to go with him to Singapore. Anandan narrated, 'She used to give solo dance performances and also prepare dance dramas. She had prepared a very ambitious dance drama named *Kaveri Thantha Kalaichchelvi*, which was so popular that she had invitations to perform it from all over the world. She made plans for a world trip and gave dates to everyone. Everything was finalized and even the advance money received. At that time there was a world Tamil conference organized in Singapore. MGR was the chief guest, and he asked Jayalalithaa to go with him, suggesting that she could proceed on her world trip from there. Jayalalithaa refused, even though MGR was then the chief minister. MGR insisted that she go with him and defied her to go on the world trip without his permission. She was so upset and so angry that she cancelled the entire trip and paid all the artistes their dues. She even dissolved the dance troupe. She did not want to beg MGR for permission.'

~

R.M. Veerappan on the other hand sees Jayalalithaa as the manipulator and oppressor in that relationship. He recounts, 'The '71 Assembly election was won because during the last stage I saw to it that MGR led the campaign though Karunanidhi was reluctant. At the victory celebration, the cadres came with two garlands – one for Karunanidhi and another for MGR. Our man is missing! He has left for Nepal with this lady, dressed as a Muslim. He comes back, and she prompts him to ask for a ministerial berth that Karunanidhi has not cared to give him. A man who is a kingmaker, why should he stoop to that level? Karunanidhi said, "You leave films and then come." Till then MGR never had a desire to hold any political power or offices. She provoked this enmity between MGR and Karunanidhi so that she could spend more time with him.'

Veerappan's view seems rather far-fetched – MGR was in his fifties, too old to be influenced by someone less than half his age. And the split in the DMK was bound to happen. MGR's popularity was growing by leaps and bounds, and Karunanidhi felt eclipsed and threatened, even though it was MGR who had got him the chief minister's post after Annadurai's death. After the 1971 elections MGR had also become a member of the Legislative Assembly, besides being the treasurer of the DMK. And he was prone to ask too many uncomfortable questions in public. Karunanidhi expelled him from the party for indiscipline.

One week after his expulsion, on 18 October 1972, MGR announced the formation of a new political party – Anna Dravida Munnetra Kazhagam. MGR now became more deeply involved in politics, and with that came a parting of ways between Jayalalithaa and him.

For Jayalalithaa this was in a way liberation and she moved on to act with other actors.

~

It was then that she formed a friendship with the Telugu star Shoban Babu, who was much younger than MGR. It developed into a serious relationship, according to her unfinished memoirs. Her friends at that time were aware that she was in love with him, wanted to marry him and settle down to a normal life like other women. Her schoolmate Chandini and her husband Pankaj Bhulani say that when they were invited for lunch at Poes Garden Jayalalithaa showed them a huge album with pictures of her marriage ceremony with Shoban Babu. Chandini says, 'It was a pukka Brahmin marriage with punditji and ceremony. She said, "He is such a wonderful person. I am so happy." She blushed like a bride and I could see she was happy.'

But the album remains a mystery – no one else claims to have seen it. Other sources say that the marriage never took place. According to her friend Srimathi, 'She knew that Shoban Babu was already married and had a teenaged son. But he charmed her. I was introduced to him. He was a very charming man. I think what attracted her to him was that he was very intelligent and well read. She could discuss books with him. Shoban Babu was a man of few words as she was, but spoke sensibly like her. She was never the flirtatious kind and was particular about the company she kept. She did want to marry him in the traditional Iyengar fashion. Probably like Vijayanthimala, who married Dr Bali, a married man. She asked for my help to make an Iyengar thaali – mangalya sutra. She asked me to attend her quiet wedding that would take place in her house. She said she had already purchased sarees from Nalli. On that day, early morning at six, she called me and said the wedding was cancelled and hung up.'

When Srimathi asked her later what had happened, Jayalalithaa indicated that there was some objection from Shoban Babu's wife.

Anandan doubted if she had plans to marry him at all. But he agreed that Jayalalithaa was fond of Shoban Babu, who was a constant visitor to Poes Garden when Anandan was her PRO. There were rumours that it was MGR who thwarted her wedding to her lover. Anything could have been possible with MGR, said Anandan.

Whatever the reason for the abrupt end to her affair with Shoban Babu, the fact that she had written about her relationship with him turned into a whip with which her political opponents lashed her. They projected her as a cheap woman, not worthy of being associated with a person like MGR.

A sickened and shattered Jayalalithaa retired from films at the peak of her glory and became a total recluse. RMV must have exulted at Jayalalithaa's self-imposed retirement. But he could not have known that she was not destined to fade away into oblivion.

Political Debut

The All India Anna Dravida Munnetra Kazhagam (AIADMK) party conference was organized on a big scale at Cuddalore, south of Pondicherry, and the whole town thronged to hear the star speaker who was to give her maiden political speech, which she had written herself. They mainly came to see a pretty face, and were instead treated to an impressive, fiery oration.

In the star-spangled politics of Tamil Nadu this was a new glamorous entry that raised many eyebrows. On 4 June 1982, Jayalalithaa had joined the ruling AIADMK party and became a card holder by paying one rupee. At Cuddalore she was taken round the streets in a carnival-type procession which the DMK described in its party paper as the 'Cuddalore cabaret'.

What made her take this first step into the political world? People who knew her said she was intellectually accomplished, had little in common with people from the film world and wanted to make the right use of her talents. She herself said it was her wish to be 'of service to the people'. What remained unsaid was there were no other options left to her after her failed love affair and dipping fortunes in the film world.

She now sought to revive her relationship with MGR, who had become chief minister of Tamil Nadu for the second time. They had been estranged for nearly ten years. She realized MGR alone could give her the break she needed. Politics attracted her but she was aware of what politics entailed. The DMK seized on her remark that she had joined politics to 'serve the people' to make lewd comments, to the effect that Jayalalithaa had offered her body to serve the people, so the youth of Tamil Nadu should come forward to avail of her offer.

~

Many in the party had come to believe that she was out of MGR's life when they parted in 1973. How did the rapprochement come about, after nearly a decade?

The man who was most shocked was of course R.M. Veerappan, now a cabinet minister in MGR's government.

He came to know later that when MGR was on an official visit to the US, Jayalalithaa also happened to be there for treatment for her obesity. A common friend arranged a meeting between the two. One meeting was apparently enough for her to change the leader's heart.

RMV's fear was that, as a member of the party, she would not be a mere wallflower. She was ambitious. She would not be content with just parading as the AIADMK's banner of glamour, or being the party's 'elegant sweetmeat that serves to attract votes like flies' as the Tamil saying goes. She was full of confidence in herself and her capabilities. She said in an interview to a national English weekly, 'I am not a person to be taken lightly.'

And she flaunted her closeness to MGR to make people believe that she was his chosen heir. From then on it became RMV's mission to malign her growing reputation so that his leader was 'protected' from being 'consumed by the evil'.

Solai, a veteran journalist and for some time political speech writer for Jayalalithaa, recalls that it was MGR who decided to bring her into politics.

He recalls, 'Because of his duties as the CM, MGR could not attend public meetings like before. When Jayalalithaa, on her own, renewed her contact with him, it was a godsend to MGR. MGR needed someone to attract the crowds and to counter Karunanidhi, who had gone on a spree of vitriolic attacks on him at his public meetings. MGR decided to make use of her for public meetings. He asked me to train her to speak. She instantly scored. The DMK was startled by the crowds that came for her meetings. She was capable of facing Karunanidhi's barbs with effective repartees. All the district AIADMK secretaries were ready to build her up. The whole party went behind her. After *thalaivar*, it will be Amma, they came to believe. Then she was made the party's propaganda secretary. RMV, S.D. Somasundaram and a few others in the party started actively working against her. But all the district secretaries and party workers were behind her. All their mischief failed in the end.'

Solai adds, 'MGR was fond of her, that was obvious, and people thought it was natural if they had physical intimacy. But they never showed that intimacy in front of people. Both remained dignified.'

Jayalalithaa was clearly confident that she would be able to tackle her detractors in the AIADMK as long as she had the trust of her mentor MGR. She said to a magazine that her relationship with MGR was special. 'Our relationship is very peculiar. Although he is so much older than me, every spare moment on the sets, we would spend talking to each other, discussing every subject under the sun. We used to talk about science, philosophy, literature. Both of us are deeply interested in classical music, astrology and astronomy. We have so much in common.'

She went on to say, 'He is everything to me. He is my father, mother, mentor, friend, philosopher and guide. He is my anchor. He will never let me down. He never lets down anyone who believes in him.'

Of course, she did not say 'he is also my lover', but the party cadres thought he was and that made her more special and lovable to them. They, who referred to MGR as Annan or elder brother, came to call her Anni – wife of elder brother.

~

When MGR made her the party's propaganda secretary her stature and importance grew manifold. She very consciously set out to 'de-glamourize' her appearance, perhaps in an attempt to wipe out the stigma attached to her as an actress. It was a signal that she was serious about her political role. Solai says that he never saw her gaudily dressed. She hardly wore any jewellery. She always wore the simple white sari with the AIADMK party border. Even so, she looked stunning and the crowds yearned to see more of her.

She had a magnetic presence, and when she attacked Karunanidhi in her hard-hitting speeches, the crowds roared their approval. She had an effective tactic at public meetings, and took to addressing questions to the crowd: 'Would you agree with Karunanidhi's malicious talk? Will you say yes to him?' The crowds would respond with a resounding 'No!' Praising MGR's noon-meal schemes and other development plans and his goodness and generosity, she would appeal to the audience, 'I am asking you; you tell me. Aren't you on the side of *puratchithalaivar*?' The crowd would reply with a thunderous 'Yes!' Her trailblazing trips across Tamil Nadu became a great success and was carefully watched by the *sakunis* in the party, who noted that her trips were arranged and organized in the same grand style and pomp reserved for MGR.

She did not stop with giving speeches. She gave the impression that her mandate from MGR was absolute. The AIADMK party headquarters buzzed with activity and Jayalalithaa's office schedule was meticulously planned, to encourage party workers to come in hordes to make representations and seek her guidance in solving their problems. She forwarded the petitions to MGR with her recommendations. She took it upon herself to look into administrative lapses in the party, made surprise visits to noon-meal halls and pulled up errant workers. MLAs who did not visit their constituencies but spent their time visiting MGR's Ramavaram Gardens residence were divested of their party posts. Senior members who missed party meetings were sent show-cause notices. People came to believe she did everything with MGR's consent.

Inevitably, a hate campaign against her began to brew. Senior party members were worried at the speed with which her power was growing, and that this novice party member might soon be given a cabinet post, but MGR had other views. He needed someone smart in Delhi who could mediate between him and the Centre. Jayalalithaa spoke excellent English. She was fluent in Hindi too. On 24 March 1984 he announced that Jayalalithaa had been nominated for the Rajya Sabha. The seat given to her in the Rajya Sabha was Number 185, the same that C.N. Annadurai had occupied when he was an MP in 1963.

Jayalalithaa stole the scene wherever she was. Her maiden speech at the Rajya Sabha was widely acclaimed for its clarity of diction and elegant prose. Khushwant Singh, a fellow Rajya Sabha member, gushed that here was a beauty with brains. Even Prime Minister Indira Gandhi was impressed.

MGR now wanted Jayalalithaa to meet Indira Gandhi. Solai, who had also been sent to Delhi by MGR to be with Jayalalithaa, describes the meeting: 'Congress was in alliance with the DMK. Our proposal was that Congress must have an alliance with the AIADMK. Jayalalithaa was told to impress this point on the PM. Jayalalithaa was given only ten minutes but they spoke for thirty minutes. Indira Gandhi was so impressed that when we were returning she sent Moopanar, Tamil Nadu Congress leader, on the same flight to broker the alliance.

'But after the meeting with Indira Gandhi, Jayalalithaa did not at once report on it to MGR, as she should have done since she had been deputed by him. MGR was naturally anxious about the outcome. When we were returning from Indira Gandhi's house I told her, please speak to the leader about the meeting. She said "that will be done" a little carelessly. But she didn't. MGR called me to ask what had happened. We departed the same day for Chennai and I asked her on the flight, "Didn't you tell *thalaivar* about the visit?" She said, "We are anyway meeting in person now. I thought we could convey it all then." This behaviour of hers, taking him for granted, sent out a wrong signal to MGR.'

She seemed to be becoming too big for her boots. The senior members around MGR kept stoking the cinders to ultimately create a conflagration.

Whether it was to pacify her detractors or to rein in Jayalalithaa, MGR announced at the party's general body meeting that he was removing Jayalalithaa from the post of propaganda secretary.

MGR could see that the prominence he had given to Jayalalithaa had virtually split the party into two. His trust in her was slowly eroding. Or so it seemed.

Upheaval

On 5 October 1984, the bottom fell out of Jayalalithaa's world. MGR suddenly fell ill – he had suffered a stroke and lost his speech, and was rushed to Chennai's Apollo Hospital. Jayalalithaa was shocked to hear that he was struggling to survive in the ICU.

Fearing the political fallout if the public and the Opposition came to know of it, the top brass of the AIADMK decided that no visitors must be allowed, especially not Jayalalithaa. Hearing that they were even planning to beat her up if she came to the hospital, Dr Pratap Reddy, the chief of Apollo, advised her to stay away.

Soon MGR was shifted to New York's Brooklyn Hospital for treatment. It is intriguing to learn from reliable sources that she was, till even a few months before, desperately trying to get married to MGR. According to Solai, 'She tried her best to get the relationship legalized. When he first became the chief minister she pestered him to marry her. But it did not happen. After MGR became CM the second time, around 1983, she decided to get married at Mugaambikai. She called me one day and said, "We have to go somewhere tomorrow. Get ready to come with me." Soon after, MGR called me and said, "I won't be in town for a day tomorrow, go to Poes Garden and please manage her." When I went there Jayalalithaa was in a very cheerful mood. We have to wait for someone, she told me. We were waiting till twelve o'clock. It was past the scheduled departure of the West Coast Express in which we had to leave. MGR never turned up. I presumed there was a plan to go to Mugaambikai and get married. She must have pressurized him. But MGR left town with his wife Janaki and could not be contacted. Jayalalithaa realized that she had been duped. In a rage, she started throwing things and breaking them. Later MGR told me that Jayalalithaa had pestered him to marry her and he had said yes. It was like cheating her, but he never thought about it seriously.'

~

Jayalalithaa's detractors made the best of MGR's absence to strengthen their crusade against her. They even deprived her of the VIP room at Tamil Nadu House in Delhi allotted to her by MGR. She had no access to MGR. She was kept totally in the dark about his condition. And she was suddenly divested of her post as deputy leader of the AIADMK parliamentary party, a post given to her by MGR.

In retaliation, Jayalalithaa unleashed a vitriolic diatribe against the 'coterie of deadwood' in the AIADMK who were out to humiliate and sideline her. Journalists lapped it all up. Such sharp language and expression of impassioned accusations against the hierarchy made for great headlines. She spoke in fluent convent English to the eager English media correspondents who thronged her door, so that the whole nation would know the kind of farce being staged in Tamil Nadu.

She did not stop with that. She uttered words that would later come back to haunt her.

'If what I suspect is true…if MGR's mental faculties are not really alright, and he is being held prisoner by these clique of people…' she was reported as saying. As she lashed out at MGR's 'dubious mental alertness' and MGR's wife Janaki's 'questionable marital status', her enemies were carefully faxing every word to Brooklyn.

She visited Delhi and discussed the political situation in Tamil Nadu with some central leaders and ministers. This provided more grist to the mill and her foes spread the story that she was striking a deal with the Congress leaders to overthrow the AIADMK government.

While MGR was still recuperating in America, parliamentary elections were announced. Rajiv Gandhi, who succeeded Indira Gandhi after her assassination, decided to face the electorate in December 1984. The

AIADMK, an ally of the Congress, decided to have the Assembly elections along with the general elections, though their leader was absent from the scene. RMV firmly believed that the AIADMK would win because of the sympathy wave both for the dead Indira Gandhi and the ailing MGR. But he did not want Jayalalithaa anywhere near the campaign.

Following Rajiv Gandhi's intervention, Jayalalithaa was allowed to campaign. Solai, who was with her, says she worked her old magic on the crowds, and they cheered loud and long when she kept saying at every public rally, 'The leader is well. He will come back.' The party won with a thumping majority.

MGR returned after a month and a half and walked briskly to the waiting car after waving to the thousands of admirers cheering and weeping at the sight of him – their god was back home restored to health.

But Jayalalithaa was not there to welcome him home – she hadn't been told that his plane would land at the St Thomas Army runway and she waited at Meenambakkam airport.

Punishing Treatment

Contrary to Jayalalithaa's fears, MGR came back mentally and physically fit except for a speech impediment. But though she tried desperately to see him, he showed no signs of wanting to see her. The intimacy that he had once shared with her now seemed like a distant dream.

It was clear that he was angry with her. Making her wait was his way of punishing her for transgressing the limits in his absence. MGR always believed in keeping the press at bay and was never in favour of his party workers giving press interviews. She had broken this hallowed edict when he was critically ill in a hospital several thousand miles away. Though she was provoked, she had erred in making the internal bickering of the AIADMK the subject of torrid public controversy and ridicule, which the DMK exploited to the hilt. MGR was also furious about her comments on his wife Janaki's marital status – that was crossing all limits of decency.

Jayalalithaa knew that if she got a chance to meet him MGR would melt. And so it was. When he returned from Japan via Delhi after a course of speech therapy, she managed to meet him there. It must have been an emotional reunion, as was evident from MGR's swift actions when he reached Chennai. On 5 September 1985, exactly a year after she was divested of the post of propaganda secretary, Jayalalithaa was reinstated. But she was not allowed to campaign for local body elections. Since MGR also did not campaign, the party lost heavily to the DMK.

In a way, this went to prove that for an electoral victory Jayalalithaa's presence made a big difference. MGR was concerned about the reverses and decided to revive his fan clubs to boost his popularity. He arranged for a mammoth conference of his fan clubs at Madurai. MGR's wife Janaki understandably disliked Jayalalithaa, and strongly resisted her re-entry into her husband's life. But to show the public that all was well MGR travelled with both of them in a plane to Madurai.

Jayalalithaa was now in a buoyant mood. She was the one who flagged off the huge procession of fans. On the concluding day she addressed the conference before MGR did. She presented MGR with a six-foot silver sceptre polished in gold. She touched MGR's feet and got his blessings. The crowd burst into rapturous applause. It was expected that MGR would make an important announcement – appointing Jayalalithaa the head of the MGR Fan Club. But he said nothing. After the function, MGR departed with Janaki, without even looking at Jayalalithaa. According to those who witnessed the scene, she stood stupefied, too shocked to believe that he would humiliate her thus, and that too in the presence of scores of party workers who believed that she was close to the leader and therefore called her Anni – brother's wife.

A week after her return from Madurai, she swallowed her anger and hurt pride and wrote an extremely emotional letter in Tamil to MGR, covering six foolscap pages. She pleaded, 'Please forgive me if I have hurt your feelings. I will not talk to anyone about Janaki. I was hurt so I must have said something. I was so upset by what happened in Madurai that I called my friend Sasi and blurted out my feelings. I will not hereafter open my mouth. Forget my behaviour and please don't be angry with me. Who else is there for me? Where will I go leaving you? Am I not your own Ammu? I write this with my countless kisses. It is more than a week since we met. Please allow me to meet you at least tomorrow. Please do not punish me further. Don't you still understand that my love for you is boundless? There is no change in that. It will not till my death. I love you so much. I desire you.'

~

The friend that Jayalalithaa was referring to was one Sasikala.

During MGR's hospitalization in the US, Sasikala, who hailed from Mannargudi, had taken over the running of the house in Poes Garden and had become an emotionally exhausted Jayalalithaa's confidante. She was the wife of Natarajan, a state government employee, who must have seen the advantage of his wife befriending Jayalalithaa even before the latter plunged into active politics.

Sasikala used to videotape events and ran a video shop in Poes Garden from where Jayalalithaa got movie cassettes to watch at home. She managed to gain entry into Poes Garden, probably by convincing Jayalalithaa that she needed someone to take care of her, and she could be her housekeeper and caretaker.

On her return from Madurai Jayalalithaa gave vent to her anger and hurt by confiding in her new friend. Obviously her words were relayed to the AIADMK supremo.

It is hard to believe that Jayalalithaa, known to be a proud woman, could cringe and plead before anyone, even if it was MGR. But the letter, which mysteriously became everyone's property in MGR's coterie, lays bare the heart of a desperate, frightened woman.

Jayalalithaa was clearly afraid of the future. She was well aware that MGR was dying, and he had not yet given her an authoritative post that would silence her opponents. Without a strong position in the party, she imagined that Janaki, his wife, could mock her with impunity. The humiliation was too much to bear.

With that emotional letter she no doubt hoped to move the old man's heart enough to give her the political power that would enable her to face the rough weather after he was gone. The name MGR carried magic. She needed it to win the hearts of the people. It was a woman's survival tactics to safeguard her position from the wolves around her, before it was too late, and to legitimize her claim as MGR's political heir.

MGR's heart stopped beating during the early hours of 24 December 1987. He died as he wished to – still in office, still the leader of his people, with his mental faculties intact till the last day. It was never his intention to name his successor, nor was he concerned about the storm his departure would create.

After MGR

'MGR is no more.'

It was a stunning blow to her. He had departed, leaving her in the lurch. In a daze she summoned the driver and rushed to Ramavaram Gardens, MGR's residence, but when she reached there she was refused permission to enter the house. She got out of the car and banged on the door with her fists. When the door was opened at last no one would say where the body was. She ran up and down the front and back stairs several times but all the doors were firmly slammed on her face to prevent her from having a glimpse of the dead body of the man who was not only her mentor but with whom she had had such a close, emotional association.

Eventually she was told that his body had been taken away through the back door and driven to Rajaji Hall. She got into her car with her heart pounding and instructed the driver to race there. At Rajaji Hall she rushed to the body and firmly planted herself at the head. MGR lay supine, neatly dressed in his full-sleeved shirt, fur cap and dark glasses – his trademark attire.

One can imagine her feelings on seeing the lifeless body of the matinee idol who had promised Sandhya, her mother, that he would take care of her dear Ammu. She did not shed a tear. She did not wail. She stunned the onlookers and mourners by standing vigil by MGR's body for two days – thirteen long hours the first day and eight hours the second day. She willed herself not to give way to physical exhaustion.

But the mental and physical torture came from other sources. Several women supporters of Janaki's stood near her and began stamping on her feet, driving their nails into her skin and pinching her to drive her away. But she stood undaunted, swallowing the humiliation and her pride, obstinately remaining where she had taken position. She seemed oblivious of her surroundings. But there must have been one question hammering her brain – what now? She was thirty-eight, single, left in limbo by the very man, now lying lifeless, who had brought her into politics with promises of a great future ahead. She, who had been looked upon by the party cadres as a natural successor to their beloved leader, was now a non-entity, fighting to have a glimpse of the departed leader. It was not in her nature to take defeat lying down.

She followed the body as it was placed in the gun carriage, trying to place a wreath on the body and join the funeral procession. The soldiers on duty helped her by giving her a hand to get into the carriage. There were at once angry shouts from behind and she saw MLA Dr K.P. Ramalingam advancing menacingly towards her. Suddenly she was assaulted – hit on the forehead by Janaki's nephew Deepan, who pushed her out of the carriage. She was hurt and bruised and shocked beyond words. Disgusted at the insults hurled at her by Deepan and Ramalingam – they called her a prostitute – she decided not to attend the funeral. She was driven home in her Contessa, escorted by soldiers.

The news spread like wildfire, sending shock waves among the party cadres. Her bruised spirits must have soared as party workers and several leaders, including MPs and MLAs, started pouring in to see her. They swore to stand by her in her claim to be MGR's successor as party leader. Many among the cadres openly said, 'We want a charismatic leader. Jayalalithaa is the only person with charisma.'

She felt assured that even though MGR had not nominated her as his successor, her standing among the people had not diminished, and they would decide in her favour. But there was no immediate need for an election. The AIADMK had won the elections with a comfortable majority. And the next elections were two years away.

Ninety-seven MLAs of the AIADMK signed a memorandum supporting Janaki and submitted it to S.L. Khurana, the Governor, who then invited Janaki to form the government. Janaki was sworn in as the chief minister on 7 January 1988. She was required to prove her majority on the floor by 28 January.

On that day there was absolute pandemonium in the Assembly on account of the Speaker showing open support to Janaki's side. Several members angrily protested against this open flouting of rules. Suddenly some goondas entered the house and started beating up the pro-Jayalalithaa group and the Congress MLAs. During the rampage someone alerted the police. For the first time in the history of the Tamil Nadu Assembly, the police entered the legislative house and lathi-charged MLAs. In the midst of all this fracas, the Speaker announced that the confidence motion was won by the government.

When Jayalalithaa was informed about the rumpus in the Assembly she knew there was no time to waste. She issued a statement that democracy had been murdered and appealed to the Governor to dismiss Janaki's ministry immediately. The protesting AIADMK MLAs, along with the local Congress members, met the Governor and gave a detailed report of what had transpired. The Governor in turn sent his report to the Centre, recommending that the situation in Tamil Nadu demanded the dismissal of the government and the proclamation of emergency. The Centre accepted the Governor's recommendation.

The turning point that Jayalalithaa was hoping for had come sooner than she had expected.

Strength to Strength

President's rule was imposed in Tamil Nadu. According to the constitutional requirement, Assembly elections had to take place within six months.

The AIADMK was split into two groups – one led by MGR's widow Janaki, supported by stalwarts like R.M. Veerappan, and the other by Jayalalithaa. Her great strength, Jayalalithaa believed, lay in the support of the party rank and file. They were there at her gates at Poes Garden even before their venerated leader's body was laid to rest, rushing to show their solidarity and affection for her in her hour of distress and humiliation.

That day she was in no mood to meet anyone, but

she went to the balcony to thank them. At the sight of her, their voices reached a crescendo in unison – 'Long live [Vaazhga] our leader! Hail future chief minister of Tamil Nadu!' For the first time since MGR's death, her tears flowed. She folded her hands and said, 'Please don't give me such titles. I do not care for either wealth or positions. I shall only carry forward what the leader had assigned me to do with your help.' She told them that when she was planning to leave political life, it was MGR who, placing her palm on the picture of his mother Sathya, had forced her to take a vow that she would not quit politics.

~

Her claim to the leadership of the AIADMK was based almost entirely on the argument that MGR wanted it that way. The strong emotional symbolism of MGR making her take an oath over the photograph of his deceased mother was not lost on the party rank and file – and it also served to place her firmly in the 'MGR lineage'. (Not surprisingly, R.M. Veerappan later said that the whole incident was a lie, that it had never happened.)

Jayalalithaa now set off on a whirlwind tour, addressing public meetings in all the districts of Tamil Nadu. The newspapers reported that after MGR no other political leader was capable of drawing crowds as she was. With every meeting, her confidence grew and so too her strength. RMV and his friends were petrified about the possible outcome. So they did what they were good at. They went on a vicious campaign, calling her names, describing her as a woman of low morals and easy virtue. Tales were spun around her private life. That she had frankly written about her relationship with Shoban Babu was repeatedly brought up in public. But she refused to be cowed down and hit back with her own abuses and vitriolic attacks on the DMK and the Janaki faction of the party. She even accused Janaki of having poisoned the last glass of buttermilk that MGR had drunk the night he died.

As the crowds increased at Jayalalithaa's campaign tours and the tone of her speeches made her sound like a leader in her own right, the senior leaders who had until now supported her began to have doubts about her. They felt that she was too domineering. Many of them left her and joined the others in attacking her.

~

The 1989 Assembly election results were telling. Since the AIADMK was split into factions, the pro-AIADMK votes were split, enabling the DMK to come back to power with a majority, after a political limbo of thirteen years. Janaki, who contested from Andippatti, her husband's constituency, suffered a humiliating defeat. Many of her candidates lost their deposit and her side won just one seat. And Jayalalithaa, whose side won twenty-seven seats, became the leader of the Opposition.

The shock of her defeat brought about a fundamental change in Janaki's attitude towards Jayalalithaa, whom she had bitterly resented for years. She accepted the 'people's verdict with humility' and declared she was quitting politics. She met Jayalalithaa and told her that her faction would merge with Jayalalithaa's group and that Jayalalithaa would therefore be the leader of the party. With the merger, the popular two-leaves symbol of the AIADMK was given to Jayalalithaa.

~

Karunanidhi, now chief minister, realized that he could not take Jayalalithaa for granted. He knew that to nip the challenge in the bud he would have to drive her out of politics. A case was foisted on Jayalalithaa and her aide Natarajan for allegedly defrauding people. It was said that the deposit money collected before the Assembly elections from the ticket seekers who in the end did not get tickets was not refunded; and when they demanded the money back, Natarajan had threatened to kill them. Police harassment became so harsh and relentless that at one point Jayalalithaa threw up her hands and said she was resigning from the legislature. She even wrote a letter to the Speaker but it is said that her party workers persuaded her not to send it. However, the media reported that she had resigned, while the Speaker announced that she continued to be the leader of the Opposition.

What followed was bizarre. When the budget session began on 25 March 1989, Chief Minister Karunanidhi, who held the finance portfolio, stood up to read his budget speech. Before he could start, a point of order was raised by the Congress that the police had acted undemocratically against the leader of the Opposition, Jayalalithaa, which amounted to a breach of privilege of a member of the house. Karunanidhi, as minister of home, was responsible for the action of the police, and so sought the permission of the house to discuss it.

Jayalalithaa quickly stood up and alleged that at the 'instigation' of the chief minister, the police had acted against her and her telephone was tapped. She also charged the chief minister with misuse of power to deny her democratic rights and urged the Chair to take up immediately for discussing the motion of breach of privilege against the chief minister and the police commissioner. The Speaker said that he would not permit a discussion on the privilege motion as the budget had to be presented by the chief minister. Pandemonium broke out as, shouting in protest, AIADMK members occupied the well of the house, and there were counter shouts from the treasury benches. When Jayalalithaa repeated that the person charged with criminal acts should not be allowed to present the budget, Karunanidhi allegedly made a crude remark about Jayalalithaa, which was of course expunged from the records, referring to her relationship with Shoban Babu. An angry AIADMK member charged at Karunanidhi, making him lose his balance. His spectacles fell to the ground and cracked, which brought several DMK ministers rushing to protect him. Missiles flew from both sides and mikes were pulled out and used as weapons. An AIADMK member tore the pages of the budget. Chappals and books landed on Jayalalithaa's head. The Speaker adjourned the house; the chief minister was escorted out by his party workers while the mayhem continued.

The *Sunday* magazine reported, 'With the battle becoming even uglier, Jayalalithaa attempted to leave the House. It was here that a member of the DMK tried to stop her and pulled at her sari as if he was trying to strip her. By now Jayalalithaa had fallen on the floor and was struggling to get up. It took a hard chop on his wrist delivered by a doughty member of the AIDMK and a few shoves to set her free. A visibly shaken and sobbing Jayalalithaa was escorted out of the House by AIADMK legislators.'

Filled with rage and humiliation, Jayalalithaa left, swearing like the infuriated Panchali that she would never step foot inside the Assembly 'until conditions are created under which a woman may attend the Assembly safely'. She may well have added to herself, 'till I enter the house as a chief minister'.

From then on Jayalalithaa sought to exploit this ugly incident to her advantage, with a concerted effort to play upon people's sympathy and use the attack on her as a metaphor for attacks on a woman's honour and modesty in general.

Creating History

When Karunanidhi came to power in Tamil Nadu it was expected that he would try to whip up anti-Delhi passions among the public on the Sri Lanka question. Any such agitation would target the stern military measures that the Indian Peace Keeping Force (IPKF) was pursuing in northern and eastern Sri Lanka. The connection between the Liberation Tigers of Tamil Eelam (LTTE) and Tamil Nadu's political groupings became abundantly clear when MGR was away in the US for three months. During that period, the IPKF decided to militarily tackle the LTTE. Unable to get in touch with MGR, who sympathized with them but did not support the demand for Eelam, the LTTE desperately appealed to Karunanidhi for political help. MGR's demise was therefore expected to drive the LTTE closer to the DMK. Delhi, on its part, had been trying to push the LTTE militarily in an attempt to prepare the ground for their unconditional surrender.

Karunanidhi, who had always tried to project himself as a true Tamilian – as opposed to the Malayalee-born MGR or the Karnataka Brahmin Jayalalithaa – sympathized with the Sri Lankan Tamils as being 'blood of our blood', and saw the emotional potency of the issue. He had already raised the question: 'If the Centre can support the Palestinian struggle for a homeland, why does it not back the movement for a Tamil Eelam?'

When he came to power in 1989, it became the Tamil Nadu government's official view. Armed Lankan Tamil militants belonging to rival groups roamed the streets of Tamil Nadu, where they brazenly fought their brawls and gunfights. There was general public apprehension at the speed with which the groups, especially the LTTE, were spreading their networks all over the state with open encouragement from the DMK and its government. The DMK and the pro-LTTE groups were outraged at the IPKF operations in Jaffna and 'the army excesses'. With Karunanidhi constantly complaining that they were responsible for butchering the Lankan Tamils whom they were supposed to protect, V.P. Singh's government at the Centre withdrew the IPKF.

The DMK was an ally of V.P. Singh's government and also a part of it. V. Gopalaswamy, a DMK member of Parliament, made a clandestine visit to Jaffna for a fortnight, without a passport and a visa, to meet the LTTE leader Prabhakaran. The AIADMK under Jayalalithaa clamoured for Karunanidhi's resignation and appealed to the Centre to dismiss the DMK government that had proved to be a danger to the security of the nation. The Centre never took her seriously.

At the end of 1990 V.P. Singh's government fell, and Chandrashekhar became the prime minister. The Tamil Nadu Congress joined Jayalalithaa to appeal to the Centre to dismiss Karunanidhi's government to save Tamil Nadu from the LTTE threat. Prime Minister Chandrashekhar visited Tamil Nadu and met Jayalalithaa at her residence with his cabinet colleagues. He avoided meeting Karunanidhi. Karunanidhi must have guessed what was in store but remained defiant. Finally, the Centre invoked Article 356 and dismissed Karunanidhi's government.

The dismissal came as a big boost for Jayalalithaa, who considered it a personal victory. She came to an understanding with the Congress for seat-sharing for the approaching Assembly elections.

Meanwhile, political uncertainty at the Centre came to an end when Chandrashekhar's minority government fell, necessitating parliamentary elections. Tamil Nadu was therefore to hold the Lok Sabha elections along with the Assembly elections.

Karunanidhi prepared to go to the people and ask for justice. But events were to take an unexpected turn that would completely upset his calculations. In May 1991, during his election campaign, the Congress president Rajiv Gandhi was assassinated by an LTTE suicide bomber at Sriperumbudur, thirty-eight kilometres from Chennai. Jayalalithaa too was on a hurricane campaigning tour. When it was known that the LTTE were behind the assassination her immediate reaction was 'Didn't we warn you?'

Even before the Jain Commission report on the assassination indicted Karunanidhi for having created an atmosphere conducive for terrorists to operate in Tamil Nadu, the people of Tamil Nadu blamed him for it and expressed their anger by voting him out of power. In both the Lok Sabha and the Assembly polls that followed, the DMK crashed to a humiliating defeat.

Jayalalithaa of the AIADMK was voted to power in Tamil Nadu with a massive mandate. History had been made. She became the first elected woman chief minister of Tamil Nadu. It had been a hard and often cruel journey for her, defying the blatantly sexist politics that tried to break her back at every stage. It was a doubly unique triumph for Jayalalithaa, because she, a Brahmin, was heading a Dravidian party.

Madam Chief Minister

It was Jayalalithaa's hour of triumph. The AIADMK's decisive victory would silence those in the party who had done their best to destroy her. She had proved that after MGR she was the face of the party, the one who could pull in the votes. On 24 July 1991 she took the oath of office as chief minister of Tamil Nadu in the name of god, at the Centenary Celebration Hall of Madras University. And as she was leaving, Sengottaiyan, a newcomer to the cabinet, fell at her feet. Other junior ministers went further and prostrated themselves full length on the floor as if before their deity. A new cult of leader worship had been initiated.

And the male world that had tried to put her down was now at her feet! She looked resplendent in her new outfit – a cape over her silk sari, which became her dress code for the next five years. There was speculation that she wore a bulletproof vest beneath that voluminous cape.

Bureaucrats were charmed by her pleasing manners, her elegance, her impeccable English and the meticulous homework she did before every meeting. They were impressed too by her vision, her plans for the state, her grasp of complex issues like the LTTE menace, and her tenacity in tackling them. And she did not mince words when her views were at divergence with those of her ally, the Congress at the Centre, whether on the Cauvery water dispute with Karnataka, the reservation policy or on restoring to Tamil Nadu the Katchatheevu island, which had been ceded to Sri Lanka in 1974, affecting the livelihoods of the state's fishermen.

Her new-found self-confidence may have arisen from her feeling that she was finally liberated from MGR's clutches – this victory was hers, and hers alone.

But now, she also began to be increasingly intolerant of criticism, especially of the news reporters who failed to speak about her achievements but were ready to blame her for anything that went wrong.

~

Perhaps her 'Great Dip' at the Mahamakam temple tank at Kumbakonam on 18 February 1992, when forty-eight pilgrims died in a stampede, marked the beginning of her break with the Fourth Estate. To her, the day was particularly significant because it was also her birthday, and she went by the advice of astrologers who predicted that the maha dip would ensure a great future for her. The entire police force was deployed to provide her Z-category security. A bulletproof glass enclosure was built for her bathing. The devotees' ranks had been swelled by the crowds drawn there more by their curiosity to see her than by the auspicious confluence of constellations. Suddenly, the parapet wall of an old building on which a large number of people were leaning gave way under their weight. There were hardly any policemen around to handle the panic and stampede that ensued – all of them had left with the chief minister just before that.

Jayalalithaa was shocked, but did not seem to think the stampede deaths had anything to do with her visit. The astrologers did not dare tell her that it was an inauspicious beginning.

The attitude of the AIADMK and its government towards the press was already evident within a month of her coming to power. When the Tamil weekly *Kumudam* wrote an editorial comparing the dispensations of MGR and Jayalalithaa, which contained a mildly critical remark, a mob ransacked its office and beat up a few workers. The party believed that it was necessary to project their leader as an unimpeachable superpower.

The next case of intimidation came in 1992 when the *Nakkeeran* magazine alleged that the government had ordered the phones of some persons to be tapped. The editor and publisher were arrested and cases filed against them, and the *Nakkeeran* office was attacked by AIADMK party workers. Even speeches made on public platforms drew retribution – many Opposition party speakers were arrested for making 'vituperative attacks couched in vulgar language'.

～

The deification of the 'Revolutionary Leader' – *Puratchithalaivi* as she was now called – was soon fully under way. Party members started tattooing Jayalalithaa's image on their bodies. Every announcement, every new project and scheme became her personal edict, and came accompanied by her outsize photograph. The government of Tamil Nadu had become the government of one person – Jayalalithaa. Towering cutouts of Jayalalithaa greeted her wherever she went. A carpet of flowers, a few inches thick, was laid for her when she went to inaugurate the de-silting of a temple tank in Madras. Posters appeared, depicting her as Durga, the goddess Meenakshi, even the Immaculate Virgin Mary.

Side by side with this culture of sickening sycophancy grew a culture of ruthless brutality towards anyone who questioned her diktat, including bureaucrats and professionals. Chandralekha, the smart IAS officer who ventured to demand clarification about the government's decision to disinvest its SPIC (Southern Petrochemical Industries Corporation) shares at rock-bottom rates, was one such victim. Acid was thrown on her face and it was rumoured that the perpetrators acted with Jayalalithaa's approval, though this was never legally proved. Chandralekha was hospitalized for months and later resigned from the IAS.

Subramaniam Swamy, president of the Janata Party, and former union minister was attacked by AIADMK party workers when he went public with his accusation of Jayalalithaa's involvement in the TANSI land scam and filed a case against her. It was reported that she summoned her party aides and screamed at them: 'Is there none amongst you dhoti-clad fellows to silence this man?'

K.M. Vijayan, a leading Chennai lawyer who challenged the AIADMK's bill to retain 69 per cent reservation, was beaten up severely on 21 July 1994 and in hospital for several months.

The fear psychosis created by the AIADMK

under Jayalalithaa's leadership was not the only thing people began to talk about. Soon rumours began to fly around of rampant corruption, especially the audacity with which her close friend Sasikala and her relatives reportedly went about acquiring land and material. Sasikala and her relationship with Jayalalithaa undermined Jayalalithaa's reputation even within the party. The party, from seniors to the cadres who had feared a vacuum in the party after MGR's death, had been relieved by her success. Now the seniors were worried about their future and the cadres were bewildered – all because of a handful of people who had come from nowhere and were becoming increasingly dominant.

The Woman Who Knew
Too Much

The relationship between Jayalalithaa and Sasikala has not only been a mystery, but has also been responsible for a lot of resentment among those who were once Jayalalithaa's most faithful supporters. Jayalalithaa, who had distanced herself from her only brother, her relatives and friends, now declared that Sasikala was her *udanpiravaa sagothari*, a sister 'though not born from the same womb'. Party workers believed that Sasikala and her entourage at Poes Garden had erected an iron curtain that kept them away from their '*thalaivi*'. They felt their requests for appointments and their personal letters no longer reached her. She had stopped coming to the party office, and stopped meeting the district secretaries who would inform her of ground realities. Amma had changed.

What was it about Sasikala that made the aloof and reserved Jayalalithaa trust her so completely? Jayalalithaa had longed for a normal life of marriage and children, which she was not destined to have. Now at least there was a friend who heard her woes with sympathy. Who did not question her actions. Who did not argue with her. Who had taken on the responsibility of running her house and who did not advise her on matters of state. It was annoying, therefore, when people said that Sasikala was behind her many political decisions. It was not only an insult to her as the chief minister but also utter rubbish.

~

One reason given for Jayalalithaa's crushing defeat in the May 1996 Assembly elections was the excesses committed by Sasikala and her coterie. In a lengthy interview to *The Hindu*, after her humiliating defeat, and after Sasikala had been dramatically arrested by the Karunanidhi government and sent to jail for violations of the Foreign Exchange Regulation Act (FERA), Jayalalithaa categorically denied the allegations and staunchly defended her friend. 'Sasikala never functioned as an extra-constitutional power centre. People must understand that a politician also needs someone to look after his or her home. A male politician has a wife at home and a woman politician has a husband or brother to take care of her personal matters. I have no one. It is only because Sasikala stepped in to take care of my household that I was able to devote my full attention to politics.

'After MGR's death, I went through a very traumatic phase and I had no one at home here to help me with anything. So at that time Sasikala and Natarajan offered to help. So I accepted their help in good faith. They both came to live here.'

Her long-time and loyal household staff were replaced by the couple's own people. They also brought in the Grey Cats security personnel for her personal safety. Natarajan was given charge of handling her finances. In Jayalalithaa's own words, 'But very soon Natarajan overstepped his limits and I did not like his high-handed ways and interference. So I asked him to leave my house. But Sasikala opted to stay with me. This was one full year before I became the chief minister. Natarajan has not stepped into this house again. Sasikala has sacrificed her whole life in order to be with me and give me moral support and take care of me. In fact, there was an occasion when she saved my life. It is because of her that I am alive and was able to lead the party to a tremendous victory in 1991.'

It is strange that Jayalalithaa could be so naive as to think that Sasikala would remain incommunicado with her husband living in the same town, just because Jayalalithaa had asked him to get lost.

~

The rumour mills gave a malicious spin to her relationship with Sasikala, alleging that they were lesbians. A letter supposedly written by Jayalalithaa to her personal physician about it was leaked to the press. The doctor and Jayalalithaa both denied that there was any such letter. But the DMK leaders often employed this weapon to malign her. When asked about this by Simi Garewal in her chat show, Jayalalithaa said she just ignored such stupid allegations.

But it had become all too evident that Sasikala's relatives, popularly known as the Mannargudi Mafia, were growing increasingly dominant and controlling her movements as well as her visitors and phone calls.

After Sasikala entered Jayalalithaa's life, most of those who had been loyal to her gradually drifted away.

Sasikala had become Jayalalithaa's alter ego.

A seasoned journalist believes that it is a financial web in which both are caught. 'Sasikala is now a woman who knows too much. Jayalalithaa cannot wish her away.'

The Writing on the Wall

Apart from the rumours and controversies around Sasikala, new problems confronted Jayalalithaa on the political front, both in Tamil Nadu and at the Centre. The Congress, Jayalalithaa's ally at the Centre, was initially pleased with the immediate steps she took with great determination and severity to contain the activities of the LTTE in Tamil Nadu, the assassins of their dear leader Rajiv Gandhi. She did this not to please the Congress, but because of her personal conviction. But the Congress was taken aback and extremely annoyed when, at her party conference in Madurai in July 1992, she made an audacious observation that the massive mandate she received from the people was due to *her* charisma alone, and not due to the sympathy wave following Rajiv Gandhi's assassination. Enthusiastic AIADMK cadres had erected a huge cutout of hers in Madurai, 135 feet high, soaring into the skies. It was a symbol too of the fact that she was fast losing sight of the ground beneath her feet.

Unlike MGR, who was shrewd enough to realize that it would be detrimental to antagonize the ruling Congress in Delhi and its local members in Tamil Nadu, Jayalalithaa believed that her charisma, her popularity alone, would carry her forward in her path to glory. The governmental machinery receded to the background, the officials became mute observers, and party members, even ministers, covered their mouths in reverence and fear when they went near her to speak.

~

MGR, who had the reputation of slapping reporters who had displeased him or catching them by the collar, had taught her that the press was not to be trusted.

After a brief honeymoon, she too shunned the press and more than a hundred defamation cases were filed against papers and journals that were 'unfriendly' to her. She even declared that she did not care a damn what the papers said – after all, the voters did not read them.

Alienating the press, gagging the voice of dissent, was a big blunder. Soon, she would take on the Governor, and when her differences with him reached a crescendo, there was not a single paper that would support her.

Once the alliance with the Congress ran into trouble, Jayalalithaa unilaterally declared that the AIADMK alliance with the Congress was over. When the local Congress members protested – like the DMK in the Opposition – that their complaints about the rampant corruption in the government were ignored by the Governor Bhishma Narain Singh – the Centre brought in a new Governor, Dr Chenna Reddy.

It looked as if Chenna Reddy had come determined to 'rein in the lady'. There was a confrontation and a war of words at every point, from clearing files that needed the Governor's signature to the appointment of vice chancellors. Then Jayalalithaa threw a bombshell in the Assembly, in answer to the criticism that she never made the customary calls on the Governor at Raj Bhavan. She said it was because he had misbehaved with her during her visit to Raj Bhavan and he was now annoyed at her being outraged and offended by his behaviour. His opposition to her was only a cover-up for his behaviour. The house was aghast. The Opposition and the press were quick to say that she was indulging in her usual theatrics – she was, after all, a former actress, with questionable morals.

When Chenna Reddy met the press in Delhi he said there was a breakdown of law and order and rampant corruption in Tamil Nadu and therefore the Centre should dismiss the government. Jayalalithaa lost no time in effecting the adoption of a resolution by the Tamil Nadu Assembly, seeking to move the Government of India for the recall of the Governor. And demanding the amendment of Article 155 of the Constitution, to the effect that the Governor must be appointed in consultation with the chief minister. No discussion on the Governor's conduct was allowed. *The*

Hindu's editorial called it 'a grave breach of propriety'.

The very next day the Madras High Court, in a landmark judgement, dismissed the writ petition filed by her against the Governor's order sanctioning her prosecution on corruption charges, clearly indicating that those holding high office were not exempt from the accountability demanded of the ordinary citizen.

The writing on the wall was clear, but she obstinately refused to read it.

By now she had totally alienated the press, and they carried frequent reports that the party coffers needed to be filled to fight the next election, and that corruption was rampant in every government department.

One of the several cases in which Jayalalithaa was charged and found guilty in the lower court involved her government amending the state environmental laws that prohibit builders from constructing more than two floors in the hills. This was done reportedly to facilitate one Rakesh Mittal, the builder of Pleasant Stay Hotel, who had built seven floors.

The government that had earned the reputation of being secretive and inaccessible now also began to be described as a 'cash and carry' government. And by the end of the fourth year, her regime became synonymous with goonda raj.

The Big Fat Wedding

The Srirangam Iyengar Brahmin community to which Jayalalithaa belonged was aghast at the news that Jayalalithaa had adopted Sudhakaran, Sasikala's nephew, who belonged to the Thevar community, far below the Iyengars in the caste hierarchy. The news came as yet another blow to those in her party who were already upset at the growing dominance of Sasikala's family. Then came another shock: Jayalalithaa announced the wedding of Sudhakaran to Sathyalakshmi, the granddaughter of Sivaji Ganesan, her former co-star and MGR's professional rival. 'I want you to think of this as a wedding in *your* house.

All of you must participate in it and make it a success,' she announced to her party workers.

Why did Jayalalithaa decide to adopt this boy for whom she had no particular fondness? Indeed, after her electoral defeat within months of the wedding she disowned him and dropped him like a hot potato. What pressure was she under to take this completely unexpected step? To her party workers it looked like a sign of her growing weakness and vulnerability. Perhaps it was a decision of convenience – perhaps to consolidate the votes of the Thevar community, which formed a sizeable chunk in the southern districts, or to safeguard her fortune by transferring a part of it in her foster son's name. Or perhaps she was excited by the idea of a wedding in the house, conducted by her as the foster mother of the groom – like being in a film in which she had the role of queen mother.

The wedding proved to be a massive political blunder, discrediting her within the party as well as with the public. The sheer ostentation, the vulgar display of wealth, watched by even the rural population on the pro-DMK Sun TV, the channel owned by

Karunanidhi's grandnephew, made Jayalalithaa an easy target – accusations of amassing wealth at the expense of ordinary people came thick and fast.

The wedding also drew public attention to Sasikala and her family – who was this mere caretaker at Poes Garden who had risen to such a position of prominence?

~

The wedding took place in September 1995. Preparations to accommodate two lakh invitees to the wedding began months earlier, with blatant misuse of government machinery. Workers from the city corporation and state electricity board, among others, were deployed.

The route of the wedding procession was transformed into a tinsel town with massive arches, viewing galleries, lanterns and decorations that outdid the most elaborate film sets. There were horses, dancers and fireworks – of the kind one saw at royal weddings in films. Sudhakaran and his bride too were dressed like a prince and princess, with a smiling, bejewelled Jayalalithaa, the queen, looking on benevolently. Brightly clad young women threw fragrant jasmine buds and rose petals as Sasikala and Jayalalithaa walked past in all their glittering finery.

The wedding was rumoured to have cost one hundred crore rupees, though Jayalalithaa rubbished that claim in an interview later. One particular photograph of Sasikala and Jayalalithaa, decked with jewels from head to toe, was published in many magazines. It may have been distributed by the DMK, and the photograph may even have been tampered with – but it remains the most unforgettable image from that wedding.

In the elections the following year, the people who had adored her as their Amma turned away from her en masse. In a rare interview to *India Today*, soon after her stunning defeat in the 1996 elections, she admitted that 'the wedding that she performed of her foster son was one great blunder which she will regret forever'.

~

In the months before the elections Jayalalithaa's popularity had plummeted sharply, but she seemed quite unaware of it. A steady stream of corruption charges against her and her cabinet ministers continued to be filed in the courts, but she simply blamed the media for spreading false rumours. The DMK, led by the shrewd Karunanidhi, well aware of the change in the public mood, was gearing up for the elections confident of ousting Jayalalithaa.

The Tamil Nadu Congress had been alerting the Centre about the growing unpopularity of Jayalalithaa's government and the humiliating slights they had faced from her in spite of being an electoral ally in the 1991 elections. They suggested an alliance with the DMK for the coming elections in May 1996. But the Congress high command ignored them, and in March 1996 announced an alliance with the AIADMK for the Lok Sabha and Assembly elections.

The Congress high command had its own reasons. The DMK had been blamed after Rajiv Gandhi's assassination for creating an atmosphere conducive to the LTTE's terrorist plot. Prime Minister Narasimha Rao did not imagine his decision would spark off a conflagration in Chennai. Watching the burning effigies of the prime minister in the wide lawns of Satyamurthi Bhavan, G.K. Moopanar, president of the Tamil Nadu Congress, declared that the party would split. On 30 March he met the DMK chief Karunanidhi and formed an alliance under the banner of his new party, Tamil Maanila Congress (TMC), while Rao's Congress went ahead with its alliance with Jayalalithaa.

Jayalalithaa believed that aligning with the Congress might help her and Sasikala to get out of the tangle of Enforcement Directorate investigations. Sasikala was the chairperson and director of JJ TV, which was charged with FERA violations. T.T.K. Dinakaran, Sudhakaran's brother, was booked under COFEPOSA by the Enforcement Directorate, also for FERA violations. The Tamil media carried numerous reports on how Sasikala's relatives, exploiting her closeness to Jayalalithaa, were on a land-buying spree, and listed the various buildings and marriage halls that her brothers and nephews had bought, all grossly undervalued and said to be benami transactions.

Matinee idol Rajinikanth too joined the opposition campaign, openly declaring that if Tamil people voted Jayalalithaa back to power, even the gods would not forgive them. It was repeatedly telecast on the Sun TV channel.

As the elections approached, Jayalalithaa's misdeeds took centre stage, while her considerable achievements were ignored. During the five years of AIADMK rule the state had become No. 2 in the country in terms of adult literacy, at 68 per cent second only to Kerala. Nobody remembered the determination with which her government had flushed out the LTTE from Tamil Nadu and restored peace and normalcy. Police stations manned entirely by women were opened and no caste or communal clashes occurred during her regime.

~

When the 1996 Lok Sabha and Assembly election results came in, Jayalalithaa was astounded. The

DMK–TMC–Left combine won all the thirty-nine parliamentary seats in the state. The DMK came to power in the state with an absolute majority while the AIADMK won just four out of the 234 seats in the Assembly. Even Burgoor, Jayalalithaa's constituency, which she had pampered and nourished with great care, had rejected her. Within a month Sasikala and Dinakaran were arrested and jailed for FERA violations. This was just an indication of what was to come. She was now at the mercy of the DMK government, under Karunanidhi. He would move heaven and earth to destroy her. Worse, humiliate her.

Political Vendetta

In the DMK election manifesto, Karunanidhi had vowed to attach the wealth of Jayalalithaa and her associates, hold enquiries into various allegations and mete out punishment to the guilty. Now that he was in power he had to deliver on those promises. He had the judicial sanction – the courts, while rejecting the anticipatory bail pleas submitted by Jayalalithaa, also admonished the Karunanidhi government for delay in taking action. The public mood had transformed from silent acceptance during Amma's rule to anger against blatant corruption.

But Karunanidhi also knew that if his government

was seen to be victimizing Jayalalithaa, the strategy could boomerang. He worried that if she went to jail it could set off a sympathy wave in a state where such events are known to provoke mass hysteria.

But Jayalalithaa's arrest had become a political necessity. His own party cadres were baying for blood and growing impatient. He had at one time feared that she would be a difficult opponent for his not-so-astute son Stalin. But now he thought that behind bars and bogged down with the endless stream of cases filed against her, she would be finished for life. He discussed the pros and cons of sending the AIADMK leader to jail with his cabinet on 5 December, and the decision was made.

On the afternoon of 6 December, Justice C. Shivappa of the Madras High Court rejected seven anticipatory bail applications filed by Jayalalithaa, including the one in the Rs 8.53 crore colour television scam for which she was ultimately booked and arrested.

~

When Jayalalithaa heard that her bail applications had been rejected she realized her arrest was imminent. On the morning of her arrest, one can imagine her feelings as she bathed, draped herself in a maroon sari and stood before the gods in the puja room. She must have wondered if even the gods had forsaken her for sins that she had not consciously committed. All the corruption charges were untrue as far as she knew – and grossly exaggerated. Her auditors had assured her that everything was properly accounted for and within legal parameters.

How was she going to prove her innocence? The puja room was filled with the fragrance of incense sticks and jasmine. Did memories of her father come back to haunt her – that handsome man who had died in despair, after having squandered his considerable wealth? She too had come to power with an unassailable mandate, but had squandered it all. It was not merely the loss of power – it was the humiliation and loss of dignity that must have tormented her. Did she wonder if she should end it all? She had tried a couple of times before. We cannot know. It is more likely that, as she had done so many times before, she had pulled herself together and decided to fight back.

When she finally appeared at the portico, where her followers had silently assembled, the dull pallor of her face was visible. She raised her right hand to make a 'V' sign, and said, 'Nalai namathe!' Tomorrow is ours!

Aided by two policewomen she stepped into the police van. At the Madras Central Jail remand prisoner No. 2529 quietly entered her cell. Within minutes Sun TV beamed the arrest. As the raids in her house and various other places followed, Sun TV beamed them again and again so that the man in the street could see the amazing collection of jewellery and other valuables belonging to the former chief minister who had also been an actress.

With over 2500 AIADMK party activists taken into custody before her arrest, protests were muted – one person committed suicide and a few buses were burnt.

Karunanidhi told reporters that the arrest was not political vendetta. 'We only followed the court's directions. Sasikala, who ran an ordinary video-cassette shop, managed to acquire property worth over Rs

1000 crore in less than five years. Her ration card and voter identity card reveal beyond doubt she was with Jayalalithaa in Poes Garden.' No reporter ever asked how the government had arrived at the figure of the alleged worth of property owned by the two.

~

Even before her arrest, when Sasikala and several AIADMK ministers were arrested, Jayalalithaa announced on 27 August 1996 that she had nothing hereafter to do with Sasikala, whom she had all along described as her *udanpiravaa sagothari*. She also declared that her decisions were hers alone and were never taken because she was pressured by any one person or a family. Sasikala, in spite of being renounced by Jayalalithaa, proved to be remarkably loyal, and refused to speak a word against her.

The evidence collected by the Crime Branch in the colour TV case showed that in December 1995 Jayalalithaa had called for the file relating to the purchase of TV sets and fixed the price of each set at

Rs 14,500 – higher than the market rate. Considering that the order was for as many as 45,302 sets to be distributed to village panchayats, the investigating authorities argued that the government could have bargained for a hefty discount. Though there were six other cases filed against her by the state and central agencies, Karunanidhi's government picked the TV scandal to nail her – it showed her direct personal involvement in finalizing the deal.

~

When she was arrested, most newspapers predicted that with so many corruption cases against her, her political resurrection would be an uphill task. Cho Ramaswamy, writer and editor of the magazine *Thuglak*, however, predicted, 'You cannot write her off!'

Jayalalithaa was in jail for twenty-eight days and when she came out she was more hardened than chastened. It must have been a traumatic experience – she later described in graphic detail how she had suffered in the bandicoot-infested jail. But the jail wardens were deeply touched by the dignity with which she conducted herself. She never complained. She hardly spoke to any of them. She spent her time reading.

Released from jail, she now stood before the people as a woman with not a gram of gold on her person, a woman whose jewellery had been seized, assets frozen and properties attached. A woman alone, victimized in the cruel male-dominated political arena. The hearts of the people melted.

Yes, Cho Ramaswamy was right. She could not be written off. Her words 'Nalai namathe' were prophetic.

The Wounded Tigress

After her release from jail, Jayalalithaa retreated into seclusion for nearly nine months. Not out of guilt or shame – she was like a wounded tigress whose fury cannot be contained. It had to have its pound of flesh.

For her own survival, she had to save the party, which seemed to have gone into limbo. The cadres were overjoyed when she re-emerged at the party office, her ears, hands and neck bare of any ornaments, her cape discarded. 'I am still in politics,' she told them, 'because I do not want it to be written in history that the AIADMK, a party that MGR founded in opposition to Karunanidhi, was wiped out by Karunanidhi.'

The cadres wept at her words. The party could not exist without her. That was her strength. And it was important to show that she was still the undisputed leader, whom no one else in the party could challenge.

~

It was a change in the political atmosphere in Delhi that triggered Jayalalithaa into action once again. The Jain Commission report, released in November 1997, gave a jolt to the DMK, which was an ally and also a part of the cabinet of the United Front government under I.K. Gujral at the Centre. The report, which looked into the larger conspiracy behind the assassination of Rajiv Gandhi, singled out the DMK, holding Karunanidhi and his party responsible for abetting Rajiv Gandhi's murderers. The Congress party, which supported the United Front government from outside, now demanded the exclusion of the DMK from the United Front ministry, failing which it would withdraw support. Karunanidhi refused to bow out voluntarily as that would indicate that the DMK accepted the Jain

Commission findings. When the Congress sent its ultimatum, Gujral waited for four days for the DMK to resign, but when it did not, he sent in his resignation letter to the President.

The country was now headed for a snap general election. Jayalalithaa quickly calculated that the Congress had not regained its strength while the Bharatiya Janata Party (BJP) seemed to be emerging with a strength not visible before. She now engineered an alliance with the BJP in a quiet meeting with L.K. Advani, creating history in Dravidian politics. She realized it was important to join hands with a national party that had a good chance of forming the government in Delhi. By giving the BJP strong support in the Lok Sabha, she could bargain for crucial ministerial berths that would help her wade through the numerous corruption cases in which she was embroiled. If she was lucky, she might even persuade the Centre to topple the DMK government in Tamil Nadu and pave the way for her return.

Jayalalithaa's strategy was to campaign vigorously, projecting herself as the wronged woman upon whom false allegations were heaped by Karunanidhi, who had made her languish like a petty criminal in jail for twenty-eight days. It would rouse the sympathy of the people. Her campaign was also for a stable government at the Centre.

On the eve of the elections, something else happened that helped her cause. On 14 February 1998, the day the BJP leader L.K. Advani was to address a meeting in Coimbatore, a series of bomb blasts at thirteen places left at least fifty people dead. Advani escaped because of a change in the time of the meeting. The bomb blasts shook the DMK and rattled Karunanidhi because fingers were pointed at him for not taking note of the warnings given to him.

In the aftermath of the demolition of the Babri Masjid in Ayodhya in December 1992, a fundamentalist organization called Al Umma had begun gaining ground in Coimbatore. Karunanidhi ignored the frequent clashes that erupted between Al Umma activists and the police.

Jayalalithaa went to town blaming Karunanidhi's government for turning Tamil Nadu, which during her time was a 'garden of peace', into a safe meadow for terrorists and unsafe for innocent civilians. In the parliamentary elections, the DMK combine was routed, and the Jayalalithaa-led alliance bagged thirty seats, the AIADMK alone securing eighteen of them. The public seemed to have forgotten that they had sent Jayalalithaa packing two years ago.

Jayalalithaa was jubilant. She was empowered once again. The BJP, which did not have an absolute majority, depended on the support of her eighteen MPs to stay in power. This was the best time to strike a good bargain, one that would facilitate her one-point agenda – the dismissal of the DMK government on the grounds of the breakdown of law and order in the state.

When she gave 'unconditional support' to the BJP-led government she evidently expected the prime minister to instantly dismiss the DMK government, in acknowledgement of her status as an indispensable ally. For twelve months Prime Minister A.B. Vajpayee gave her the royal treatment: he surrendered to her his prerogative of choice of ministers and portfolio allocation. He encouraged her to appoint or order the sacking of senior civil servants and law officers, but he stopped short of dismissing Karunanidhi's elected government. She demanded that the 'tainted' ministers Ramakrishna Hegde, Buta Singh and Ram Jethmalani be removed. Buta Singh was removed, but not the others.

The Sangh Parivar protested loudly that Jayalalithaa had crossed the Lakshman rekha when she objected to the removal of Navy Chief Admiral Vishnu Bhagvat by the defence minister George Fernandes. She demanded that George Fernandes be dismissed. It looked as if she wanted to show Karunanidhi how powerful she was at the Centre.

But Jayalalithaa was in a great hurry. She had challenged the validity of the special courts to try her cases but the Supreme Court had given them the go-ahead. The trials would start soon and, although her lawyers said that she would come through unscathed, she was afraid that the DMK's manipulations would spell her ruin.

She then went to Delhi and 'incidentally attended' a 'tea party' at which all the Congress leaders including the Congress president Sonia Gandhi were present. It was like a blackmail message to the BJP government at the Centre – she would switch sides if her request was not met.

And so the inevitable happened. It is believed that the BJP refused to agree to the dismissal of Fernandes, and on the pretext of the government's refusal to accede to her demands, Jayalalithaa withdrew her support in 1999, and the government fell, defeated by one vote in the dramatic no-confidence motion that followed.

The Congress made a pathetic attempt to form the government, claiming to have the required numbers, but it failed to present proof. Elections were declared, but the BJP-led government was asked to continue as the caretaker government well through the Kargil war. It was a loss of face for Jayalalithaa, though she showed no sign of regret. Her action paved the way for strengthening her enemy's position.

~

That was in 1999, the DMK's golden jubilee year.

Ironically, it was the year the party was obliged to take a major policy decision that went against its ideology. Karunanidhi convened the executive council of his party to discuss the issue. The council unanimously agreed that the priority before them was to block the 'Jayalalithaa danger'. Despite the historical enmity between the DMK and the Rashtriya Swayamsevak Sangh, the executive body took the decision to support the BJP. (After the Jain Commission findings, Sonia Gandhi was maintaining a studied distance from the DMK.) Vajpayee was an old friend of Karunanidhi's from the Emergency days and, most important, had refused to succumb to Jayalalithaa's pressures to dismiss the DMK government. So in the elections that followed, the DMK would take a conscious decision to align with the BJP.

Jayalalithaa had not anticipated that the DMK would go to any length to finish her off.

Back in the Ring

After the fall of the BJP government and the announcement of fresh elections to the Lok Sabha in 1999, Jayalalithaa realized that she must pick herself up and begin the fight again. As the main architect of the Vajpayee government's collapse, it seemed inevitable that Jayalalithaa would resurrect her traditional alliance with the Congress. But when she aligned with the BJP she had made cruel remarks about Sonia Gandhi's nationality. Now she swallowed her pride and let herself be guided by expediency. She sealed an electoral alliance with the Congress. For Jayalalithaa, power at the Centre was a must to counter the DMK government's relentless pursuit of anti-corruption cases against her.

Her fans hardly understood the polemics of ideology or the intricacies of poll. What mattered to them was that Amma should be the winner in any combination. And that Karunanidhi, the villain Duryodhana, should be vanquished.

Forgetting or ignoring her word to the party cadres a year earlier that she had nothing more to do with Sasikala's family, she allotted the Periyakulam constituency ticket to T.T.K. Dinakaran, Sasikala's nephew who was under the Enforcement Directorate's scanner for FERA violations and had come out of jail on bail. Sasikala, who had been in jail for nearly two years, was also out on bail. It was rumoured that she was back in Poes Garden. She remained unseen in public for some time, but she was soon escorting Jayalalithaa on her campaign tours. The party members and cadres were disappointed, but the rumblings were muted. They probably realized that for practical reasons, as a single woman in an all-consuming political job, she needed someone like Sasikala.

She continued to draw a massive crowd at her

meetings, and the sight of them must have been like balm to her soul, proving that she still had a hold over them. If the Congress, her ally, won in Tamil Nadu it would be because of her charisma and hers alone. She never once projected Sonia Gandhi as the prime ministerial candidate. She even missed meeting Sonia with whom she had to jointly address an election rally at Vellore, on the pretext that she was held up in a traffic jam. Sonia waited, addressed the crowd and left for Delhi. *The Hindu* quoted Karunanidhi as saying, 'If the Congress indeed comes to power, Sonia Gandhi will run away to Italy unable to bear Jayalalithaa's tantrums.'

When the results were announced, she had just ten MPs on her side, while the BJP–DMK front had twenty-six.

The unthinkable had happened – the DMK was part of the Vajpayee government. There was a unique bond now between the DMK and the BJP – their common enemy was Jayalalithaa.

Murasoli Maran, Karunanidhi's favourite nephew, was the cabinet minister for commerce and industry, an important portfolio. Ram Jethmalani, whom she had antagonized in her obstinacy, was in charge of law, which was bad news for her.

Once again her future looked grim.

Casting a Spell on Destiny

The stars, she was told, could be manipulated or cajoled to change one's fate. Even numbers, said the numerologists, could distract the hand of fate. Nine is your lucky number, they had told her. So an 'a' was added to her name and she became Jayalalithaa. Yet another astrologer said green was her auspicious colour. When she took to wearing green, after she was back in power, even the officialdom went on a green spree, turning everything from ceilings to carpets, from pens to ribbons at public functions, to green. Women employees wore saris in different shades of green.

In late 1999, her horoscope indicated the

constellations in a hostile position though it was temporary, said the astrologers. But you must satiate the elements, they said. Their list of dos and don'ts was long, yet like a drowning man clutching at straws, she went along with them.

The beginning of the new millennium didn't appear to augur well. On 12 January 2000 came the news that former AIADMK MLA Mallika was convicted on corruption charges and sentenced to seven years' rigorous imprisonment. The general belief that the AIADMK was corrupt was confirmed, casting a shadow of gloom in the party office. The judgement on the TANSI land deal case was expected shortly. What would Amma's fate be? What would the future of the party be?

Nobody, not even Jayalalithaa, knew that the mood would change in less than twelve hours. The next morning Judge S. Thangaraj of the Madras High Court announced that Jayalalithaa was acquitted in the TANSI case. Jayalalithaa couldn't have been more surprised. It was surely the grace of some unknown gods. Or there was perhaps a change in the alignment of the constellations. JAYA TV jubilantly flashed the breaking news on its ticker. 'Dharma won. Malice lost' cried the headlines the next morning in the AIADMK party paper *Namathu MGR*. There was utter shock in the DMK camp. Karunanidhi and his advisers had firmly pinned their hopes on this case. The CBCID (a special unit in the Tamil Nadu Criminal Investigation Department) had charged that the land – 3.78 acres in the Guindy industrial estate, Chennai – that belonged to TANSI, a government unit, was bought in 1991–92 by Jaya Publications and Sasi Enterprises in which Jayalalithaa and Sasikala were shareholders, at a rate lower than the market price, incurring loss to the government. More important, it was a blatant misuse of power as the chief minister of the state.

Judge Thangaraj questioned the legal validity of the charge. That a government servant should not acquire government property was only a guideline, not a law. Therefore, it was not a punishable crime. Further, there was no evidence to establish the prosecution charges that Jayalalithaa schemed and misused her power to cheat the government and acquire the land. (Ultimately the Supreme Court too acquitted her, stating that the prosecution charge was weak.)

Soon, however, came a huge setback. The Special Court Judge V. Radhakrishnan, who had acquitted her in the 'coal import' scam, now indicted Jayalalithaa and her former minister Selvaganapathy, along with H.M. Pande (an IAS officer), Rakesh Mittal and P. Shanmugam, proprietors of Hotel Pleasant Stay, for having collectively conspired to violate environmental laws to build extra floors in the hotel in Kodaikanal, a hill station. They were each sentenced to one year's rigorous imprisonment.

Jayalalithaa who was present in the court was shell-shocked. When the news reached the streets, pandemonium broke out. At the party head office, the AIADMK lower-rung workers went berserk. Riots broke out through the state. Ten buses were burnt and ninety damaged. The police seemed paralysed. The violence reached its savage height when some AIADMK supporters set fire to a bus full of girl students of Tamil Nadu Agricultural University, Coimbatore, which was on its way back from Dharmapuri. Three girls, Gayatri,

Vaasanthi

Kokilavani and Hemalatha, were consumed by the flames, and sixteen girls sustained burns.

Jayalalithaa reacted like a bad loser. She accused the DMK of having planned the attack to sully the AIADMK's name before the three assembly by-elections that were approaching. Even Karunanidhi's detractors guffawed at her outrageous allegation. The AIADMK attackers had no way of hiding their faces or their heinous crime. They had informed all the TV channels about their road blockade, so that Amma would know how loyal and devoted they were to her. The incident was filmed not only by Sun TV but also by JAYA TV, and photographed and reported in graphic detail by local reporters. The AIADMK men were seen pouring petrol over the bus and setting it alight, not heeding the terrible cries of the teachers and students.

When Jayalalithaa saw the video clips and realized they were indeed her party workers, she was furious. There was no way she could speak in support of them. The government said that a CBCID enquiry would be ordered. So be it.

The memory of those poor girls haunted her. Young,

124

bright girls, born poor, studying against all odds, hearts loaded with dreams…turned into ashes because of those fools.

The soothsayers said, don't worry, some *parihaaram* – atonement – could be made. Ah, there were always ways to wash off your sins.

Appeasing the Gods

There was discord brewing in Karunanidhi's family, due to sibling rivalry between his elder son Azhagiri and his younger son Stalin, who was being groomed as Karunanidhi's successor. Azhagiri, based in Madurai, ran his own fiefdom like a local dada, and bullied the local police, administrators and even ministers.

Jayalalithaa watched this with interest, hoping that it would sully the image of the DMK. But then came another blow: the TANSI corruption case in which the high court had acquitted her, came back for retrial in the high court, on the orders of the Supreme Court. And this time, she and the other accused were sentenced to three years' rigorous imprisonment. Jayalalithaa was sure the defence had been bribed by the prosecution to deliberately bungle the case.

Now the question was, would she be allowed to contest in an election? She could of course appeal to the Supreme Court, but who knew how long it would take for the verdict to get delivered? And who knew if it would not go against her again? The Madras High Court, to which she made an appeal against the judgement, suspended the sentence but not her conviction.

She must have wondered if there was a malign force beyond her control that was working against her, if the demons were at play. She went to the Kumbeshwarar temple at Kumbakonam to propitiate the gods.

And she presented a brave face to the public. At the twenty-ninth anniversary of the AIADMK she thundered to the applauding crowd: 'There is nothing to fear but fear itself… Karunanidhi who does not have the guts to defeat me at the people's court turns to the special courts to destroy me. No matter how many Karunanidhis try, they cannot rob us of our victory tomorrow.'

Her courage and leadership at this bleak hour put new hope into the hearts of the AIADMK cadres. She made them feel that the party's future was secure, and that her personal setbacks were temporary. Then, carried away by her emotions, she added: 'If Karunanidhi is alive when I come back to power in 2001, I shall put him in prison for life.'

~

Elections for the Tamil Nadu Assembly were announced for May 2001. That there was no clarity over whether Jayalalithaa would be eligible to contest raised Karunanidhi's confidence. Jayalalithaa filed her papers from four constituencies, but the returning officers one by one rejected them, saying that the Representation of the People's Act 8, Section 3, disqualifies a person 'convicted by a trial court who has been sentenced to more than two years' imprisonment to stand for election'.

Jayalalithaa must have known that this would happen. But she also knew what she must do next. She would travel all over the state and appeal to the people. She did not waste time talking to them about issues or principles or even about her future plans for Tamil Nadu. She told them she had been wronged, she was fighting for justice and indeed for her very survival. 'Karunanidhi has deliberately planned to destroy me. I shall fling away his mask and expose his true face!' she said. She recounted to the crowds how he had heaped false cases on her, submitted concocted evidence and coerced election officials to reject all her four nomination papers. 'For me, it is the verdict of the people that is more important than all other verdicts.' Then, spreading the pallu of her sari in her hands, she pleaded, 'I stand before you begging for alms.' Many in the audience wept.

Despite being barred from contesting herself, Jayalalithaa's party won a massive mandate. She insisted that the mandate given to the AIADMK was in fact a mandate given to her to rule the state. She was elected the leader of the legislative party. And Fathima

129

Beevi, the Tamil Nadu Governor, invited Jayalalithaa
to take charge of the state. Article 164 of the Indian
Constitution gives the Governor freedom to ask any
person to become the chief minister.

Vengeance

'Vengeance is mine!' That, it soon became clear, was Jayalalithaa's main agenda.

On 30 June 2001, just weeks after the AIADMK's election victory, Karunanidhi was dragged out of his bed in his Oliver Road residence in Chennai, at about 2 a.m. The seventy-eight-year-old DMK leader was not even given time to change his clothes, it was reported. The telephone lines were cut and the house was filled with grim-looking policemen who were there to carry out Amma's orders – the same police who had stood to attention in front of the old man as long as he was the chief minister. Using the mobile phone that was at his bedside, Karunanidhi quickly called his nephew and confidant, union minister Murasoli Maran, who happened to be in Chennai. Within minutes Maran reached the house. The Sun TV crew too arrived, and the police, perhaps high on the authority the uniform gave them, didn't care that the cameras were there to record their actions. The frail and frightened man wailed 'aiyo' in pain, as he was dragged down the stairs by ten policemen, then pushed into the van. The police rudely brushed off Maran when he asked them to produce the arrest warrant; then they engaged in a scuffle with Maran as well as T.R. Balu, also a union minister, who arrived on the scene.

Sun TV knew how potent their footage was, and they played it without a break from the morning of 30 June. Even Karunanidhi's detractors among the viewers would have been shocked at the brutality of the police. Murasoli Maran must have anticipated such an eventuality and asked the Sun TV crew to be ready at all hours and at short notice. Jayalalithaa, on the other hand, had certainly not anticipated the presence of a TV crew – she had sent the police in the dead of night to carry out the arrest because she didn't want the media to witness it. Jayalalithaa underestimated the impact among the general public as well as the media, who always felt more comfortable with Karunanidhi than with her.

The incident caused an unprecedented furore, not only in Tamil Nadu but all over India. A team of the ruling National Democratic Alliance (NDA), led by the defence minister George Fernandes came from Delhi, visited Karunanidhi in the Central Jail and recommended President's rule in Tamil Nadu. But Prime Minister Vajpayee was in no mood to take a hasty step against a regime that had a popular mandate. The big casualty was Tamil Nadu Governor Fathima Beevi, whom the Centre decided to recall as 'she had failed to objectively reflect the situation in Tamil Nadu'. (Fathima Beevi had already been widely criticized for having sworn in Jayalalithaa as chief minister, when she had been barred from contesting the election.) The recall of the Governor sent a strong warning to Jayalalithaa, who then ordered the release of the two union ministers and that of the DMK chief soon thereafter.

The case against Karunanidhi, Stalin and twelve others was related to alleged financial irregularities in the construction of flyovers. The arrest was ordered on the basis of an FIR lodged by a tainted municipal commissioner.

Jayalalithaa had underestimated her opponents for whom she had nothing but contempt – they were smarter than her, they had put their heads together and worked like a team. And Karunanidhi had the support of his large family too, who would always rally round in a crisis. Jayalalithaa did not have any good advisers, so she blundered again and again, listening only to those who said what *she* wanted to hear.

The Comeback

On 21 September 2001, the Supreme Court gave the verdict she had feared: 'The appointment of Jayalalithaa as chief minister of Tamil Nadu, which took place on May 14, was unconstitutional and void.'

A frantic Jayalalithaa summoned a meeting of ministers and district secretaries at Poes Garden. She left for Raj Bhavan immediately after, with just the AIADMK flag and not the national flag fluttering from her car, and formally informed the Governor, C.K. Rangarajan, that she was stepping down and that her successor would be announced the same evening. Jayalalithaa appointed a first-time member of the Assembly, Panneerselvam, as the chief minister. A graduate and son of a poor farmer from the Thevar community, Panneerselvam was a humble man, known for his modesty. He and all the ministers who were sworn in afresh fell at Jayalalithaa's feet and sought her blessings. Amma looked amazingly calm as she accepted their obeisance.

For all practical purposes, it was she who was still the chief minister. It was said that Panneerselvam had moved into the compound of Poes Garden and all the files went for her scrutiny before he signed. In the corridors of government offices, they waited for Amma to come back.

That happened sooner than expected. By mid December 2001 the Madras High Court acquitted her and the others who had been sentenced to three years' imprisonment in the TANSI case – so now she was free to contest an election. The person most relieved was poor Panneerselvam who, like Bharata waiting for Rama's return from his exile in the forest, was waiting for Amma's return. She stood for elections and won a handsome victory. Her brief absence from the chief minister's seat was never felt.

~

Looking back, one wonders if she would want to erase from memory the autocratic rule that she unleashed for five years, which led to her fall again in 2006. She antagonized all sections of society. Students turned against her when, by a suo motu decision in the Assembly, the hundred-year-old Queen Mary's college was to be demolished, to be replaced by a new secretariat building. The plan was dropped after a huge protest by students and academics. She antagonized government employees by dismissing those who struck work for two days; the village folk by banning animal sacrifice during their temple functions; the Centre, by arresting V. Gopalasamy, an MP and ally of the NDA; the Congress party by her barbed attacks on Sonia Gandhi. The media of course was the worst hit – every paper was taken to court for 'defamation', while her followers regularly vandalized media offices. She even tried to arrest the editor of *The Hindu*. Ministers and officials were orally instructed not to speak to the media. And she kept her ministers on tenterhooks, either summarily dropping them from her cabinet or whimsically changing their portfolios.

~

She had already suffered a major setback when the Supreme Court ordered the transfer of the two disproportionate assets cases against her and four others from a Chennai special court to a special court in Bangalore. This was a result of the petition filed by the DMK general secretary K. Anbazhagan, praying for a direction to transfer the cases to a court outside Tamil Nadu, to ensure a free and fair trial as 'the public confidence in the fairness of trial was being seriously undermined'.

By 2004 when preparations for parliamentary elections were on, Jayalalithaa was isolated and out of touch with reality. The media refrained from giving her credit even for the good work she had done. She missed sight of the gathering storm, still drunk with the majority she enjoyed in the Assembly. The storm gained momentum with ease. Karunanidhi managed to form a grand alliance with secular parties, withdrawing from his alliance with the BJP which, he suspected, was moving towards Jayalalithaa. The Congress, sensing the mood of the people in Tamil Nadu, put aside the Jain Commission report and extended its hand to Karunanidhi. Now all parties in Tamil Nadu flocked to Karunanidhi. For Karunanidhi, it was not just a parliamentary election. It was a pre-run for the Assembly elections two years away.

Defeat, Not Destruction

Jayalalithaa could not believe the news. The DMK front had bagged all the forty seats in the 2004 parliamentary elections! A jubilant Karunanidhi said it was a verdict against her anti-people rule.

Jayalalithaa was badly rattled. With a speed that signalled despair, she undid most of the controversial and unpopular measures she had taken in the past three years.

It was the DMK's resurgence that haunted her. In the politics of an 'eye for an eye' she could imagine the vendetta that would be unleashed against her if the DMK won in the 2006 Assembly elections. She must now act urgently to regain her popularity that had dipped to an all-time low.

~

With admirable determination in the last two years of her term she concentrated on good governance, and demonstrated her ability as an administrator. She took up rainwater harvesting seriously and issued an order that within two months all residents in Chennai should install harvesting tanks. To curb the increasing number of deaths from consumption of illicit spurious liquor, she decided that the government would run liquor shops – TASMACs – providing alcohol at cheap rates, a scheme that also gave employment to thousands of unemployed graduates and filled the government coffers.

Her biggest hour of triumph came when on 18 October 2004 news was flashed on all the TV channels about the death of the dreaded sandalwood smuggler Veerappan, who was killed in an encounter by a Tamil Nadu police special task force in Dharmapuri. The forest brigand was wanted by the police for poaching elephants, the abduction and killing of policemen and innocent people, and destroying thousands of sandalwood trees. Among those he had abducted was the Kannada matinee idol Rajkumar, whom he had kept in captivity for a hundred days. Karunanidhi and his counterpart in Karnataka had failed in their attempts to nab Veerappan, and people had come to believe he was invincible.

When Jayalalithaa came back as chief minister in 2001, she gave full freedom and encouragement to the special task force. And when they succeeded in their mission, Jayalalithaa's stock soared.

Then she did something that jolted even her opponents. On Deepavali day, the Shankaracharya of Kanchi was arrested. Jayalalithaa was known to be an ardent devotee of the Kanchi Mutt and no one expected her to take such a bold step. The Kanchi seer was given to airing offensively anti-women views, which had angered educated women. But now he was arrested on criminal charges. Rumours abounded about undesirable activities in the mutt. The acharya, an ambitious man, was increasingly interfering in politics, and his influence was not confined to Tamil Nadu. It therefore took real guts to arrest such a powerful and influential man. The general public in Tamil Nadu, with the exception of a section of the Brahmin community, surprisingly supported her action. Even Karunanidhi applauded her when she said that everyone was equal before the law.

Before the dust settled in Kancheepuram, there was a by-election there, and the verdict would say if she was right or wrong. To her great relief and to the surprise of the rest of India, her party won the Kancheepuram seat.

~

Then came a natural disaster of terrible magnitude. On 26 December 2004 a tsunami hit the shores of Tamil Nadu, swallowed hundreds of lives and destroyed thousands of homes. Within hours Jayalalithaa's government swung into action. To the credit of her administration, it rose admirably to the challenge. The officials responded to the calamity as if it had occurred in their own houses, fully backed and directed by the chief minister. Even the hostile press praised her government for the massive effort that was put into rehabilitation and the efficiency and commitment with which she handled it.

~

As the Assembly elections neared, the public mood swung around in her favour. Even the corridors of power in Delhi were impressed. Karunanidhi, the DMK leader, was now a very worried man. How was he to unseat this woman who grew in strength after every humiliating defeat? He had to devise a Machiavellian plan. And that is exactly what he did.

The DMK Strikes Back

As campaigning began for the 2006 Assembly elections, the allies in the DMK front declared in front of the TV cameras that they had joined hands for a cause – their main aim was to 'destroy that *pombilai*', a derogatory term for women. Jayalalithaa remained unruffled, confident of her victory. The good work the district collectors had done post-tsunami under her direction had been widely appreciated, and she was confident she had an edge over her rivals.

Then the DMK took the wind out of her sails. Almost on the eve of the elections, they came out with an extraordinary manifesto: they promised rice at Rs 2 a kilo, free colour TV sets and free gas connections to those under the poverty line, and two acres of land for the landless poor. The DMK manifesto was a master stroke. Karunanidhi, who was never known to appeal to women voters, was suddenly seen as a bountiful father figure who would give them gifts as a father would to his daughter.

The DMK coalition emerged victorious in the Assembly elections, though despite the many carrots it dangled before voters the DMK failed to get an absolute majority.

Jayalalithaa's AIADMK did not do too badly: it won sixty-one seats, the single largest party after the DMK. It could have done better perhaps, had it not been for the new party, the DMDK, floated by the actor Vijaykanth, which Jayalalithaa had dismissed as 'dust'. They got 8 per cent of the votes, cutting into hers. The Congress, which won thirty-five seats, hoped to get some ministerial posts, but Karunanidhi managed to keep them away.

And so it was the DMK in full power, supported from the outside by coalition partners. Karunanidhi dramatically signed a Government Order to sell ration rice at two rupees, minutes after the government was sworn in. Within a month, distribution of free TV sets and gas connections began. But the chief minister was now more preoccupied with his own family problems.

~

Rumours had been doing the rounds for a long time that all was not well within Karunanidhi's family, and it was not because of the old sibling rivalry that Tamil Nadu was familiar with – between Stalin and Azhagiri – but the growing power of the Maran brothers, sons of his nephew Murasoli Maran.

The family discord came out in the open after the Tamil daily *Dinakaran*, owned by Dayanidhi Maran's brother Kalanidhi Maran's Sun TV network, carried a survey on who should be Karunanidhi's successor in the DMK party. The results of the survey showed that 70 per cent of the voters wanted M.K. Stalin as Karunanidhi's successor; only 2 per cent wanted Azhagiri. This was enough to ignite a riot. On 9 May

2007 supporters of Azhagiri attacked the *Dinakaran* office in Madurai, ransacked it, broke windows and doors and hurled petrol bombs, leaving two employees and a security guard of the media group dead. In its news bulletins, Sun TV directly accused Azhagiri of unleashing his goons against the group's office in Madurai and called for his arrest.

The people of Tamil Nadu, avid watchers of Sun TV, the most popular TV channel, were horrified, and the DMK soon realized that urgent damage control was necessary. Arcot Veerasamy, the state minister for electricity, let it be known that Dayanidhi Maran had reportedly threatened the state home secretary with dire consequences if he failed to arrest Azhagiri. After the DMK party sat for a meeting and condemned the 'anti-party activities' of Dayanidhi Maran, and 'authorized' its leader Karunanidhi to take action against him, the young man who had shown spectacular success within a short period as the union communications and IT minister, sent in his resignation.

Karunanidhi cleverly silenced the media by announcing that the probe into the tragic Madurai events would be handed over to the CBI as his 'own son was blamed to have been behind it'.

But it was soon clear that money and power were behind the family war. There was a sudden patch-up between the Maran brothers and the family patriarch Karunanidhi, and pictures of the united, beaming family were published in all the Tamil papers.

~

When the DMK, continuing with the same alliance during the Lok Sabha elections in 2009, won eighteen seats, Karunanidhi bargained with the Congress that came to power, to get a cabinet post for Dayanidhi Maran, and one for Azhagiri too – a man who had never crossed the boundaries of Tamil Nadu. He also got his daughter Kanimozhi nominated to the Rajya Sabha. There was now a growing uneasiness within the party at the way Karunanidhi was promoting his family.

And yet, it was the AIADMK that appeared weak after the parliamentary elections, which made it clear how important it was to have a good coalition now in Tamil Nadu to win an election, whether for the Lok Sabha or for the Assembly. Jayalalithaa's attitude towards her alliance partners, however, left much to be desired – she either ignored them or refused to be accommodating. She was also becoming more and more distant with her own party members. District secretaries and MLAs needed her counsel, but Amma was frequently absent, living in Kodanadu, her resort in Ooty.

Now or Never

Despite being leader of the Opposition, with sixty MLAs in the Assembly, Jayalalithaa now rarely attended the Assembly sessions. While her senior party leaders held the fort in the house, frequently staging walk-outs in protest against the DMK government's actions, she was busy tracking the growing clout and wealth of the Karunanidhi clan.

Now suddenly, Stalin's son Udhayanidhi, and Azhagiri's son Dhayanithi Azhagiri, became producers of big-budget films. They had not gone to any financiers or taken loans from anywhere, so where did the money come from? When Karunanidhi thundered 'Why should my grandchildren not enter films if they like?' and compared himself to Prithviraj Kapoor and Rajinikanth, she scoffed at the ridiculous comparison. Unaccounted money, administrative power, a stranglehold over the visual and print media and near total monopoly in the film world – how long would the people keep quiet?

Some insiders in the intelligence agencies fed her with facts and figures of the family's excesses and also those of the ministers. She filed this information away meticulously for later use. Then there were the complaints of unscheduled power cuts, price rise, illegal sand quarrying – the list was long and new items were getting added constantly.

~

For Jayalalithaa, the time had come to strike – it was now or never. She announced a protest meet of the AIADMK at Coimbatore, to raise questions that would shake the DMK to the core. Jayalalithaa's gamble paid off. It was clear that her authority as the leader of the

AIADMK was still unquestioned. Her party workers organized the event with admirable efficiency and enthusiasm. An astonishing crowd, estimated at eight lakh, assembled at Coimbatore. When she vowed to fight the evil forces and assured the enthralled crowd that MGR's rule would soon be back, she seemed to be the very embodiment of Kali, the destroyer of evil.

But her most audacious decision was to hold a meeting in Madurai, Azhagiri's bastion. And the crowds gathered again. They came defying threats to their lives and hers, many of them walking fifteen kilometres to see her. 'I received several threats that I will be killed if I come to Madurai,' she said in a resounding voice, 'because they say this is the bastion of anjanenjan [brave heart, as Azhagiri is called by his followers]. Is Madurai Azhagiri's ancestral property? I will not be cowed down by such threats. I am standing here in front of you and have proved who really has a brave heart,' she thundered to a cheering crowd.

Azhagiri had earlier taunted her: 'Her cadres deify her as Meenakshi, Kamakshi and Visalakshi. Can they call her Virgin Mother?'

In the run-up to the 2011 Assembly elections, the poll predictions pointed to a hung Assembly. She proved them wrong. The AIADMK, now in an alliance with Vijaykanth's DMDK, won an absolute majority on its own. The DMK suffered a humiliating defeat and was pushed to number 3 in the Assembly.

The Mother Figure

While Jayalalithaa savoured her massive victory in the 2011 elections, she must also have relished the dark days that the Karunanidhi clan went through after they were routed in the elections. Karunanidhi's protégé A. Raja, union minister in the Congress-led government, and daughter, Kanimozhi, Rajya Sabha MP, were charged in the 2G scam, arrested and sent to jail, on charges of alleged fraud and corruption. According to her, the DMK had lost ground irretrievably, and no longer posed a challenge to the AIADMK. As she declared to her party men after winning the 2011

Assembly elections, 'Don't worry about the DMK. As far as that party is concerned, it is a finished story.'

Her previous stints in power had taught her that impulsive actions of anger and vengeance would only harm her. As a result, her third term as chief minister was relatively tranquil, even though she remained unforgiving in many respects. Within the administration, she brooked no opposition, demanding that her word on any subject be considered law.

She manoeuvred public support with her array of populist welfare schemes, thanks to which 'the man in the street gets everything he needs' in the name of 'Amma'.

She projected herself as the mother figure in all her welfare schemes and election speeches. She offset any public discontent with her largesse: 20 kilos of rice free for each BPL family, mixie-grinders and fans – never mind the still-existing power shortages – and bicycles for schoolchildren, all distributed as Amma products. Amma canteens run by municipal corporations sprang up in cities, selling idlis for one rupee each and curd rice for three rupees. The Tamils believe in the old adage 'Be grateful as long as you live to the person who fed you'.

~

The 2014 parliamentary elections were approaching and that opened up new vistas, new dreams. Hoardings all over Tamil Nadu declared Jayalalithaa as prime-minister-in-waiting. She behaved like one already, making audacious decisions, though fully aware that they would not go unchallenged. She announced the release of Rajiv Gandhi's assassins who were serving life terms in jail. Now she was eyeing the moon – all forty parliamentary seats in Tamil Nadu in 2014. Were she to gain something close to it, she might well be the kingmaker – or the king.

As talk of the Third Front came up, the West Bengal chief minister Mamata Banerjee openly offered to support her for the prime minister's post when the eventuality arose. If the BJP-led NDA came away with inadequate numbers from the general election, it would have to come to her for support. Either way, she presumed, victory was hers.

She said to her party workers, 'The AIADMK can make it to the Centre and redeem this nation to a new freedom.' They believed it.

But the Modi wave that surprised the entire nation swallowed all her dreams, and though the AIADMK swept the Tamil Nadu polls, winning thirty-seven parliamentary seats, she could be neither the kingmaker nor the king.

~

But Jayalalithaa was never one to look back and regret what might have been. She lived in the present, and she was happy with her present situation – after all, hers was now the third largest party in the Lok Sabha; and she was convinced that she was now invincible in Tamil Nadu. Ah, but she had almost forgotten about the sword hanging over her head – the disproportionate assets case against her, pending in the Karnataka court. Or perhaps she thought she would be forgiven her lapses because of her overwhelming popularity among the Tamil masses and her political power. In her third term as chief minister she appeared to have consolidated and understood the art of wielding power.

In the past she had been acquitted in almost all the cases filed against her and she hoped that she would now be acquitted in the disproportionate wealth case as well. On the day the verdict was to be announced, 27 September 2014, hundreds of her party workers thronged the Karnataka sessions court, waiting to burst crackers to celebrate Amma's victory. The verdict hit her like a thunderbolt: she stood convicted, sentenced to four years in prison and a fine of Rs 100 crore.

Amma showed little of the emotion that had appeared on her face in 1996, when she was taken to prison from her Poes Garden house. Then, she had looked at those who stood before her gates and said, 'Naalai namathe.' Now she came out briefly to have a word with her loyal follower O. Panneerselvam – he would be the chief minister in her absence.

She quietly spent about twenty days in jail in Bangalore, during which period her entire cabinet and the senior party brass went on religious penances and did special pujas to almost all the deities in the temples of Tamil Nadu. She was released on bail for health reasons on 18 October, but refused to meet party members waiting to celebrate. She went into a shell, not stepping out of Poes Garden for the next eight months. No one knew what she did inside her house during that period. There were rumours that she was seriously ill.

Then came another dramatic swing in her fortunes. On 11 May 2015 the Karnataka High Court acquitted her completely in the disproportionate wealth case. It was a sensational comeback. Jayalalithaa responded with a simple statement: that the verdict gave her immense satisfaction and it proved she was innocent.

The DMK and the Karnataka government went for an appeal to the Supreme Court against the verdict, but Amma seemed least bothered. In her usual fashion, she decided she would cross that bridge when she came to it.

She was once again back in the chief minister's

seat. She was given six months' grace period to contest again. During her absence the government had come to a literal halt. She belied all reports about her failing health by launching the projects that were stalled, making sure the credit for these came to her alone. She won with an astonishing margin when she contested from R.K. Nagar, Chennai.

~

Amma doesn't quite realize how Tamil Nadu has changed since she first entered politics. There is a huge social churning going on among the youth, now exposed to the Internet and WhatsApp. New voices are rising against the long rule of the two Dravidian parties, the DMK and the AIADMK. The welfare measures have been a big hit with the lower middle class but the young now have different aspirations. When the rains poured like never before in Chennai and other parts of the state and the city was inundated by the delayed opening of the Chembarambakkam lake, the government stood paralysed for three days. The people were angry that Jayalalithaa did not rush to their assistance. The anger was still there as the May 2016 Assembly elections approached, and her opponents believed it would be reflected in the results.

~

As the campaigning gathered steam, she remained outwardly unperturbed and confident. Unlike the DMK that was desperate for allies she audaciously announced that her party would contest all 234 seats. All efforts by Karunanidhi to form a united front failed, and it resulted in a five-cornered contest: the AIADMK, the DMK+Congress, the BJP, the PMK and Vijaykanth's front that had four groups of the People's Welfare Front. Election analysts were convinced that the anti-incumbency votes would be split and that would be to Jayalalithaa's advantage. But was her vote bank intact? Was her hold on the party still as firm? Would her welfare schemes bring her back to power once again?

It would be a tough fight. Karunanidhi's son and

chosen heir, Stalin, had been travelling all over Tamil Nadu over the past year. With his complete makeover in dress and speech as a dynamic man with a modern outlook, speaking a language that the man on the street understands and appreciates, Stalin looked like a mass leader already, a fitting successor to his father, the ninety-three-year-old Karunanidhi.

~

At her election rallies, her silver Toyota Prado flying the red and black pennant of the AIADMK would arrive to thunderous applause. She would walk slowly to the canopied dais, her special cushioned chair surrounded by air coolers. This time, she did not deliver her usual rousing oration. Instead, she would read out a prepared speech before the lakhs of people who had been sitting in the hot sun from morning to see her. She would read out a list of her achievements, and also her complaints against her foe, Karunanidhi. This time, the fire and passion was missing. But the crowds did not seem to mind. Indeed, the sight of her, looking tired and aged as she travelled from one rally to another, seemed to arouse their protective instincts.

'Would they vote for again?' journalists went around asking people at her rallies. Few were prepared to give a clear answer. But many said that whether or not they would vote for her, they would always come to hear her. In power or out of power, she will always be their Amma.

Will the Stars Protect Her?

On 16 May 2016, Jayalalithaa arrived with her aide Sasikala to cast her vote at the polling booth in Stella Maris college. Exit polls had almost unanimously predicted a victory for the DMK+Congress. A reporter rushed to ask her what she thought were her prospects of winning. Jayalalithaa looked calm and impassive. Then she smiled and replied, 'Wait for three more days, you will know.' It was a knowing smile.

At Gopalapuram, Karunanidhi, leader of the DMK, after casting his vote was asked a similar question. 'The DMK will win adequate seats,' he replied. It was a modest statement, considering the fact that pollsters had predicted victory for the DMK.

The morning of 19 May saw the people of Tamil Nadu glued to their TV sets, and party workers of the DMK and the AIADMK assembled at their respective party offices. The road leading to Jayalalithaa's house in Poes Garden was getting increasingly crowded as the results started pouring in. One moment the DMK seemed to be leading, the next moment the AIADMK – the fluctuating fortunes of the two parties kept the cadres in a state of high suspense.

At Anna Arivaalayam, the DMK headquarters, signs of unease were palpable by 10 a.m. Women and men travelling from far had gathered for a celebration. When they heard that the AIADMK was leading in 124 seats, some broke down and others shook their heads in disbelief. They knew how hard Thalapathy – that is, Stalin, Karunanidhi's son – had campaigned, and they had been so confident that the DMK was going to win. Inside the building the mood was defiant. DMK supporters huddled in a room watching Kalaignar TV, the channel owned by party leaders. The channel was saying that the AIADMK was leading only in 114 seats, while DMK led in 95. They kept their hopes up all morning, refusing to read the writing on the wall.

By mid-day it was clear that Jayalalithaa was coming back to power with 134 out of 234 (elections in two constituencies, Thanjavur and Aravakurichi, were cancelled due to allegations of money paid to voters by the AIADMK). But her margin of victory at R.K. Nagar constituency from where she had contested was much less than her earlier win from there. Of all the winners, it was Karunanidhi who scored the highest number of votes – from Tiruvaiyaru. The DMK, however, could not get a majority though it won 89 seats and with its ally the Congress came out with 97 – in all as the biggest opposition the Tamil Nadu Assembly had seen so far. As Karunanidhi pointed out, the difference in vote share between the two fronts was very small. The AIADMK's was 40.8 per cent while the DMK+Congress front received 38 per cent. Dayanidhi Maran, former telecom minister and son of Karunanidhi's nephew Murasoli Maran, said, 'Mandate of people of Tamil Nadu was for the

DMK but, unfortunately, crores of money was spent by Jayalalithaa...'

Whatever the criticism and allegations, nothing succeeds like success. The people gave a decisive vote, giving Jayalalithaa the majority, making the DMK a strong opposition, and ruthlessly rejecting upstarts like Vijaykanth's front and the PMK.

Outside Poes Garden, women danced in jubilation, and the sound of drums and firecrackers filled the air. A beaming Jayalalithaa, clad in her trademark green sari, made her victory speech sitting in the porch of her residence amid a steady stream of visitors, including top officials, falling at her feet. 'I am overwhelmed by the resounding victory the people of Tamil Nadu have given us,' she said. 'My party and I are indebted to the people of Tamil Nadu for giving this historic victory.'

~

The win was truly 'historic' in the sense that after 1984, when MGR had won even while he was away in the

US undergoing treatment, this was the first time that a ruling party had won the elections and gone on to form a government for a second consecutive term.

During the campaign Jayalalithaa declared that she had no interest or ambition other than serving the people and that her life was dedicated to them. She also emphasized that she had no major tie-up with any other party 'while ten parties opposed her'. When she announced that the AIADMK would go it alone, her party men kept quiet as usual, though they worried that their leader's overconfidence may be a mistake. But evidently, she knew what she was doing. Thanks to this, she had picked and fielded her own candidates without having to meet the demands of allies. She boldly experimented with many new faces – after all it was her face, her charisma, that got them the votes. She did not hesitate to keep changing the candidates after nominating them. But there was not a whimper heard from any quarter.

Winning handsomely without the help of allies now gave Jayalalithaa a power that was awesome. As one political observer wryly commented, 'Those ever-prostrate party men are never going to get a chance to straighten their backs.'

~

An autocrat she is, no doubt. But a benevolent one, her followers add, and one who knows how to win and wield power, reaching out with special schemes to the business community, to farmers and the poor. She understood full well the impact of her social welfare schemes under the Amma brand. When the time came to vote she was confident the people would remember the Amma canteens, Amma water, Amma baby kit, Amma cement, Amma pharmacies and Amma seeds...the fans, laptops, cycles and grinders that made life so much easier for rural folk. She smiled like a goddess when she said, 'Makkalukkaaga naan, makkalukkaagavewaan' – I am for the people, only for people. You did not even have to pray to be blessed.

Though the opposition guffawed at the hype of the Tamil Nadu Global Investors Summit, organized by Jayalalithaa in September 2015, it succeeded in bringing in investors to the state, offering them tax breaks and land at subsidized cost. And she won the support of farmers to a large extent by providing 100 per cent subsidy to small and micro farmers. Free goats and milch cows for families also helped swing rural votes. Now she has announced that all loans will be waived for micro and small farmers.

It was lucky for her that the opposition was split, with each group comically aspiring for the chief minister's post. It was also her luck that the DMK has not regained its former popularity with the public after its collapse during the last election due to the DMK's alleged involvement in the 2G scam. She keeps harping too on the excesses of the DMK's family rule. Even so, the DMK was able to increase its vote share by more than 10 per cent due to the tireless efforts that Stalin undertook to revive the party. So she knows she cannot be complacent. Jayalalithaa, who spits fire at the very mention of Karunanidhi's name, is quite charming when she deals with Stalin. She apologized for the oversight when Stalin, leader of the opposition, was made to sit in the fourth row and not given prominence during her swearing-in ceremony. She explained that she was not aware that he was present, and graciously thanked him for attending the ceremony.

~

Soon after taking the oath as chief minister, her first act was to close down 500 TASMAC shops (state-run liquor shops) that were situated near schools and places of worship. She knew that this was an emotive issue, especially with women voters, and she kept the promise she had made in her manifesto as she set about ensuring that prohibition for selling alcohol would be done in stages.

Even as she got into her stride as chief minister of Tamil Nadu for the fourth time, uncertainty clouded her immediate political future. What would be the verdict of the Supreme Court in the disproportionate wealth case in which she had been absolved of guilt in the High Court of Karnataka?

At sixty-eight, she has reached a stage when such worries do not frighten her any more. She has, as she once said, waded through an inferno to reach where she has.

But the burden of carrying the party on her shoulders is tiring and frustrating sometimes. She knows encouraging a second-in-line as her political heir would be suicidal. There is no one in sight anyway. She does not know what will happen to the party after her.

She was born under the star Magam. There is a saying in Tamil astrological parlance: Magaththuppen jagaththilum illai – A woman born under the star Magam is incomparable to any other in the world. Would that star continue to protect her?

A Note on the Author

Vaasanthi is one of Tamil Nadu's best-known writers. Her books include *Cut-outs, Caste and Cine-stars: The World of Tamil Politics*, and several novels. She was editor of the Tamil edition of *India Today* for nearly ten years.

1

CRAFTED FOR MOBILE READING

Thought you would never read a book on mobile? Let us prove you wrong.

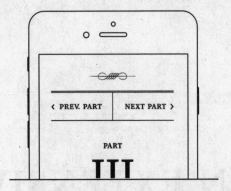

Beautiful Typography

The quality of print transferred
to your mobile. Forget ugly PDFs.

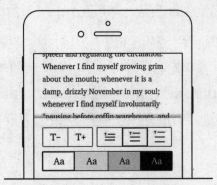

Customizable Reading

Read in the font size, spacing
and background of your liking.

2

AN EXTENSIVE LIBRARY

Including fresh, new, original Juggernaut books from the likes of Sunny Leone, Praveen Swami, Husain Haqqani, Umera Ahmed, Rujuta Diwekar and lots more. Plus, books from partner publishers and loads of free classics. Whichever genre you like, there's a book waiting for you.

DON'T
JUST READ;
INTERACT

We're changing the reading experience from passive to active.

Ask authors questions

Get all your answers from the horse's mouth.
Juggernaut authors actually reply to every
question they can.

Rate and review

Let everyone know of your favourite reads or
critique the finer points of a book – you will be
heard in a community of like-minded readers.

Gift books to friends

For a book-lover, there's no nicer gift than
a book personally picked. You can even
do it anonymously if you like.

Enjoy new book formats

Discover serials released in parts over
time, picture books including comics,
and story-bundles at discounted rates.
And coming soon, audiobooks.

4

LOWEST PRICES & ONE-TAP BUYING

Books start at ₹10 with regular discounts and free previews.

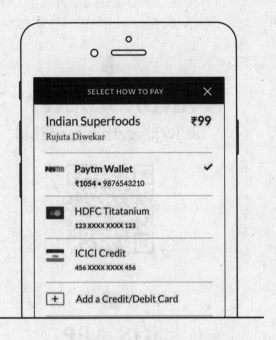

Paytm Wallet, Cards & Apple Payments

On Android, just add a Paytm Wallet once and buy any book with one tap. On iOS, pay with one tap with your iTunes-linked debit/credit card.

ENG-2

Click the QR Code with a QR scanner app
or type the link into the Internet browser
on your phone to download the app.

ANDROID APP
bit.ly/juggernautandroid

iOS APP
bit.ly/juggernautios

For our complete catalogue, visit www.juggernaut.in
To submit your book, send a synopsis and two
sample chapters to books@juggernaut.in
For all other queries, write to contact@juggernaut.in